LATIN AND GREEK WORD ROOTS, GRADE 4

Teacher Guide

INTRODUCTION

Latin and Greek Word Roots, Grade 4+ includes Latin and Greek word roots related to fourth grade and above. The program is used at higher levels and in different ways depending on student groups and ability levels.

Latin and Greek Word Roots, Grade 4+ includes 5 parts.
Part 1: Word Root Lessons
Part 2: Word Root Tests
Part 3: Word Root Search Activities
Part 4: Word Root Concentration Games
Part 5: Word Root Reading and Meaning

Latin and Greek Word Root Chart

While presenting the lessons display the word root chart related to the lessons in the classroom. There are four word charts. If possible, enlarge the charts. They are found following this introduction.

Part 1: Word Root Lessons

Thirty-five lessons present four word roots in each lesson. Lessons are organized in alphabetical order, except for the Greek root *hydr* which follows the Latin root *aqu*, both roots meaning *water*.

> Before passing out lesson 1, page 1, present the lesson on the chalkboard. The presentation helps students see that consistent Latin and Greek word parts are clues to word meanings.
> Write the following words on the chalkboard.

act - to do   **in** – not   **re** – again   **inter** - together, between
●●●●●●●●●●●●●●●●●●●●●●●●●●●●●●●●●●●

inactive
The word root *act* means *to do* something.
  • What does the word *inactive* mean?
  • The word root *in* often means *not*.
  • Yes, the word *inactive* means *not active, not doing anything.*
●●●●●●●●●●●●●●●●●●●●●●●●●●●●●●●●●●●

<u>**re**</u>**act**

- The word root *act* means *to do something.*
- What does the word *react* mean?
- The word root *re* means *again*

Yes, the word *react* means *to act or do again.* (It means that something we already know or do well we are doing again.) Present the following sentence.

She **reacted** to the good news with a smile. (She has smiled before; she is smiling **again**.)
●●●●●●●●●●●●●●●●●●●●●●●●●●●●●●●●●●●●●●●

interact

- The word root *act* means *to do something.*
- What does the word *interact* mean?
- The word root *inter* means *together* or *between*

Yes, the word *interact* means *to do something together with others.*

Tell students that learning word roots helps them understand many words. Tell them that the meanings presented in these words are found in many other words.

LATIN

act to do

act- **to do** something
● It was an **act** of bravery.
in**act**ive (**in**- *not*)- **not active;** not doing anything
● Are most healthy people **active** or **inactive?**
re**act** (**re**- *again*)- to **act again**; to respond to
● She **reacted** to the good news with a smile.
inter**act** (**inter**- *between*)- to **act together** with others
● I like **to do** things with other people; I like to **interact** with them.

Pass out the first student lesson on page 1. Help students complete the lesson. In each lesson, students study word roots, write their definitions, and write them in sentences. The sentences on the lesson card have a dot in front of them. (For extra credit have students write their own sentences for each word.) Find the lesson answers at the end of the lessons.

Part 2: Lesson Tests

Give the tests on the same day as the lesson or on other days. Students review the words and meanings prior to the test. Answers to the tests are found following the tests in Part 3, Tests.

Part 3: Word Search Puzzles

Present word search puzzles after every three lessons. The puzzles are excellent reviews, and they motivate students. Answers to the puzzles follow each puzzle.

Part 4: Word Root Concentration

The word root concentration game is played like Concentration games. Students cut out word cards and turn them over.
Then they match the cards. The student with the most cards wins the game.

Part 5: Word Root Reading and Meaning

Students practice reading the word roots and discuss their meanings. Time the students on their readings.

Drawing Masters

A drawing master is included for students to draw pictures about the word roots. Students enjoy drawing, and the drawings can be displayed in the classroom. The drawing master is in the Teacher Guide.

WORD ROOT CHARTS

Latin and Greek Word Root Chart 1
(LESSONS 1-8)

1. **act** (to do) act **in**active **re**act **inter**act
   i. **not** **again** **between**

2. **anim** (life, spirit) animal animate **in**animate **magn**animous
   i. **without** **great**

3. **aqu/a** (water) aquatic aqu**arium** aque**duct** aqua**naut**
   a. **a place for** **to lead** **explorer**

4. **hydr** (water) hydrant hydro**electric** **de**hydrate hydro**phobia**
   i. **remove** **fear**

5. **art** (skill) art art**ist** artisan arti**fic**ial
   a. **one who** **make**

6. **aud** (hear, listen) aud**ible** **in**aud**ible** audience audition
   i. **able to** **not able to**

7. **bi** (two) bi**cycle** bi**lingu**al **bio** (life) bio**logy** bio**graph**y
   i. **wheel** **language** **study** **write**

8. **cap, cept** (take, receive) capture cap**able** accept **inter**cept
   a. **able to** **between**

Latin and Greek Word Root Chart 2
(LESSONS 9-16)

→

9. | cent (hundred) | centurycent**enn**ial **bi**cent**enn**ial **per**cent
years **two years** **parts**

10. | cert (certain, sure) | certain **un**certain certi**fy** certificate
not **make**

11. | chron (time) | chronicchron**ology** **syn**chronize chrono**meter**
science of **same, together** **measure**

12. | circ, circum (around) | circle circus circum**vent** circum**nav**igate
to go **sail**

13. | con, com (with, together) | connect con**greg**ate combine comm**uni**ty
flock **one**

14. | cycl (circle, wheel) | cycle **re**cycle **bi**cycle cyclone
again **two**

15. | dec (ten) | dec**ade** dec**athlon** decimal deca**pod**
group **contest** **foot**

16. | dem/o (the people) | demo**cracy** demo**crat**ic **epi**demic **pan**demic
government **government** **among** **all**

→

Latin and Greek Word Root Chart 3

(LESSONS 17-25)

17. **dict** (speak, say)   dictate dictat**or**   **pre**dict   **contra**dict
    one who   before   against

18. **equ** (equal, same)   **un**equal   equal   equality   equi**la**teral
    not   side

19. **ex** (exit)   exit   ex**pel**   ex**tend**   ex**claim**
    drive   stretch   cry out

20. **fin** (finish, end, limit)   finish   **in**finite   define   **con**fine
    not   together

21. **flor** (flower)   flora   flor**ist**   Florida   flori**cult**ure
    one who   cultivate

22. **graph** (write, draw)   **bio**graphy   **auto**biography   **auto**graph   **biblio**graphy
    life   self   self   book

23. **hosp** (guest house)   hospital   hospitality   **host** (stranger, enemy)   hostage   hostel

24. **logy, ology** (study of, science of)   **bio**graphy   **chron**ology   **eco**logy**zo**ology
    life   time   environment   animal

25. **medi** (middle)   medial   median   **inter**mediate   Medieval   Medi**terr**anean
    between   land

Latin and Greek Word Root Chart 4

(LESSONS 26-35)

→

26. **nov** (new) novel novice **in**novation **re**novate
in, into **again**

27. **nym, onym** (name, word) **syn**onym **ant**onym **homo**nym **an**onymous
same **opposite** **same** **without**

28. **omni** (all) omni**poten**t omni**vor**e **pan** (all) pana**cea** pan**orama**
powerful **to eat** **cure** **view**

29. **ped** (foot, feet) pedal pedestrian **bi**ped pedi**cure**
two **care**

30. **pri, prim** (first) prim**ary** primitive primate prior**ity**
relating to **state of**

31. **tend, tens** (stretch, strain) **ex**tend tense intensity **hyper**tension
out **above, over**

32. **terr** (land) terrace territory **Medi**terranean terr**arium**
middle **a place for**

33. **tract** (draw, pull) tractor **at**tract **dis**tract **ex**tract
to **away** **out**

34. **uni** (one) united uniform uni**cycl**e uni**son**
wheel **sound**

35. **vis, vid** (see) vision vis**ible** **in**vis**ible** video
able to **not** **able to**

→

DRAWING MASTER

Direction: Choose words from the **lesson** to illustrate.

For each word: draw a picture, a symbol, a cartoon, or an ad, or write the word in an interesting way.

Word _____ Root(s)_____	Word _____ Root(s)_____
Word _____ **Root(s)**_____	**Word** _____ **Root(s)**_____

PART 1
LESSONS

act to do

act- **to do** something

● It was an **act** of bravery.

inactive (**in-** *not*)- **not active**; not doing anything

● Are most healthy people **active** or **inactive**?

react (**re-** *again*)- to **act again**; to respond to

● She **reacted** to the good news with a smile.

interact (**inter-** *together, between*)- to **act together** with others

● I like **to do** things **together** with other people; I like to **interact** with them.

● Say each word.   ● Underline the word roots.   ● Write each word again as one word.

<u>act</u>   in <u>act</u> ive   <u>re act</u>   inter <u>act</u>

act   inactive

● Write the complete word on the lines.   ● Write the definition.   ● Write the word in a sentence.

1. act (to do) = <u>a</u> <u>c</u> <u>t</u>

Definition   **to do** something

Sentence   ● It was an <u>**act**</u> of bravery.

2. in (not) **+** act (to do) **+** ive = _ _ _ _ _ _ _ _ _

Definition

Sentence

3. re (again) **+** act (to do) = _ _ _ _ _

Definition

Sentence

4. inter (together) **+** act (to do) = _ _ _ _ _ _ _ _ _

Definition

Sentence

anim life, spirit

animal- a **living** thing

● What is your favorite **animal**?

animate- to make **alive**; **lively**; full of **life** and **spirit**

● Her idea led to an **animated** discussion.

in**anim**ate (**in-** *without)*- **without life** or **spirit**

● Are baseballs and chairs **animate** or **inanimate**?

magnanimous(**magn-** *great)*-great; generous **spirit**, forgiving

● The **magnanimous** president was loved by all.

- -

● Say each word.   ● Underline the word roots.   ● Write each word again as one word.

anim al   **anim** ate   **in anim** ate   **magnanim** ous

● Write the complete word.   ● Write the definition.   ● Write the word in a sentence.

1.   anim (life, spirit) **+** al **=** _ _ _ _ _ _ _

Definition _____

Sentence _____

2.   anim (life, spirit) **+** ate **=** _ _ _ _ _ _ _ _

Definition _____

Sentence _____

3. in (without) **+ anim** (life, spirit) **+** ate **=** _ _ _ _ _ _ _ _ _ _

Definition _____

Sentence _____

4. magn (great) **+ anim** (life, spirit) **+** ous **=** _ _ _ _ _ _ _ _ _ _ _

Definition _____

Sentence _____

13

aqu, aqua water

aquatic- things happening in or on the **water**

● I enjoy **aquatic** sports such as swimming and **water** skiing.

aquarium (arium- a *place*)- **a place** for keeping fishes and marine plants

● Their **aquarium** has goldfish and **aquatic** plants.

aque**duct** (duct- *to lead*)- a large pipe or canal **to lead** or carry **water** over a long distance.

● The **aqueduct** makes farming possible.

Aqua**naut** (naut- *explorer*)- an under**water explorer** (diver, etc.)

● She is working as an **aquanaut**.

● Say each word.   ● Underline the word roots.   ● Write each word again as one word.

aqua tic   **aqu** arium   **aqu**e **duct**   **aqua** naut

Write the complete word.   ● Write the definition.   ● Write the word in a sentence.

1. **aqua** (water) + tic = _ _ _ _ _ _ _

<u>Definition</u>

<u>Sentence</u>

2. **aqu** (water) + **arium** (a place) = _ _ _ _ _ _ _ _

<u>Definition</u>

<u>Sentence</u>

3. aqu (water) + e + **duct** (to lead) = _ _ _ _ _ _ _ _

<u>Definition</u>

<u>Sentence</u>

4. aqua (water) + naut (explorer) = _ _ _ _ _ _ _ _

<u>Definition</u>

<u>Sentence</u>

hydr water

hydrant- a large **water** pipe for drawing **water** (fire **hydr**ant)

● Water **hydrants** are important to help put out fires.

dehydrate (**de-** *remove*)- to **remove** all **water** from

● Grapes are **dehydrated** to make raisins.

hydrophobia (phobia- *fear*)- **fear** of **water**

● I love swimming; I don't have **hydrophobia.**

hydroelectric- producing **electricity** by the action of falling **water**

● Why are **hydroelectric** power stations found near **water**?

● Say each word. ● Underline the word roots. ● Write each word again as one word.

hydrant   **hydr**o electric   **hydr**o phobia   de **hydr**ate

---

● Write the complete word. ● Write the definition. ● Write the word in a sentence.

hydr (water) **+** ant **=** _ _ _ _ _ _ _

Definition

Sentence

2.   **de** (remove) **+ hydr** (water) **+** ate **=** _ _ _ _ _ _ _ _ _

Definition

Sentence

3. **hydro** (water) **+ phobia** (fear) **=** _ _ _ _ _ _ _ _ _ _ _

Definition

Sentence

4. **hydro** (water) **+ electric =** _ _ _ _ _ _ _ _ _ _ _ _ _

Definition

Sentence

art skill

<u>art</u>- a **skill** by which one creates
- Acting, painting, writing, and composing are all forms of **art**.

<u>art</u>ist (ist- *one who*)- **one who** is **skilled** in music, literature, or any other form of **art**
- The singer gave an **artistic** performance.

<u>art</u>isan- a person **skilled** in a particular craft (carpenter, plumber, electrician, etc.)
- We called a **plumber** to fix our leaky faucet.

<u>art</u>ificial (**fic**- *make*)- **made** by **skilled** people, not by nature
- The **artificial** flowers are made of plastic.

- Say each word.   • Underline the word roots.   • Write each word again as one word.

art   **art ist**   **art** i san   **art** i **fic**ial

- Write the complete word.   • Write the definition.   • Write the word in a sentence.

1. art (skill) = _ _ _

Definition

Sentence

2. art (skill) + ist (one who) = _ _ _ _ _ _

Definition

Sentence

3. art (skill) + isan = _ _ _ _ _ _ _

Definition

Sentence

4. art (skill) + i + fic (make) + ial = _ _ _ _ _ _ _ _ _ _

Definition

Sentence

aud — hear, listen

audible (ible- *able to*)- **able to** be **heard**
- His voice was barely **audible**.

in**aud**ible (in- *not*)- **not able to** be **heard**
- His voice was **inaudible**.

audience- a group of **listeners**
- The **audience** clapped loudly.

audition- a **hearing**
- The actor was given an **audition** for a part in the play.

- Say each word.   • Underline the word roots.   • Write each word again as one word.

aud ible   **in aud ible**   **aud** i ence   **aud** i tion

- Write the complete word.   • Write the definition.   • Write the word in a sentence.

1. **aud** (hear, listen) **+ ible** (able, to) = _ _ _ _ _ _ _

Definition _____

Sentence _____

2. **in** (not) **+ aud** (hear, listen) **+ ible** (able to) = _ _ _ _ _ _ _ _ _

Definition _____

Sentence _____

3. **aud** (hear, listen) **+** ience **=** _ _ _ _ _ _ _ _

Definition _____

Sentence _____

4. **aud** (hear, listen) **+** ition **=** _ _ _ _ _ _ _ _

Definition _____

Sentence _____

bi two

bicycle (**cycl**- *wheel*)- a light vehicle with **two** large **wheels**
● How do you think the **bicycle** got its name?
bilingual (**lingu**- *language*)- able to use **two languages**
●I am studying a second **language**; I will be **bilingual.**

bio life

biology (**logy**- *study*)- the **study** of **life**.
●My **biology** class has posters of interesting plants and animals.
biography (**graph**- *write*)- one's **life** story **written** by another
●He is reading a **biography**, the life story of his favorite baseball player.

●Say each word.   ●Underline the word roots.   ●Write each word again as one word.

bi cycle   **bi lingu**al   **biology**   **biography**

● Write the complete word.   ● Write the definition.   ●Write the word in a sentence.

1. **bi** (two) **+ cycl** (wheel) + e = _ _ _ _ _ _ _

Definition

Sentence

2. **bi** (two) **+ lingu** (language) + al = _ _ _ _ _ _ _ _ _

Definition

Sentence

3. **bio** (life) **+ logy** (study) = _ _ _ _ _ _ _

Definition

Sentence

4. **bio** (life) **+ graph** (write, draw) + y = _ _ _ _ _ _ _ _ _

Definition

Sentence

cap, cept
take, receive

ac**cept**- to **receive**; to agree to
- He **accepted** the invitation to the birthday party.

inter**cept** (inter- *between*)- to come **between**; to **take** before arrival
- He tried to **intercept** the football pass.

capable (**able**- *able to*)- **able** to **receive** knowledge; clever
- She is a **capable** mechanic.

capture- to **take** charge of
- The police **captured** the person who robbed the bank.

- Say each word.   • Underline the word roots.   • Write each word again as one word.

| ac **cept** | **inter cept** | **cap able** | **cap** ture |

- Write the complete word.   • Write the definition.   • Write the word in a sentence.

1. ac **+ cept** (receive) = _ _ _ _ _ _

Definition

Sentence

2. **inter** (between) **+ cept** (take, receive) = _ _ _ _ _ _ _ _ _

Definition

Sentence

3. **cap** (take, receive) **+ able** (able to) = _ _ _ _ _ _ _

Definition

Sentence

4. **cap** (take, receive) **+** ture **=** _ _ _ _ _ _ _

Definition

Sentence

cent hundred

century- a period of **100** years
- We live in the twenty-first **century**.

centenn**ial** (**enn**- *years*)- happening once every **100 years**
- The United States celebrated its **centennial** in 1876.

bicentenn**ial** (**bi**- *two*) (**enn**- *years*)- happening once every **two hundred years**
- The United States had its **bicentennial** in 1976.

percent (**per**- *parts*)- number of **parts** per **hundred**
- Twenty **cents** is twenty **percent** of a dollar.

- Say each word. • Underline the word roots. • Write each word again as one word.

cent ury   **cent enn** ial   **bi cent enn** ial   **per cent**

- Write the complete word. • Write the definition. • Write the word in a sentence.

1. **cent** (hundred) + ury = _ _ _ _ _ _ _

Definition

Sentence

2. **cent** (hundred) + **enn** (years) + ial = _ _ _ _ _ _ _ _ _ _

Definition

Sentence

3. **bi** (two) + **cent** (hundred) + **enn** (years) + ial = _ _ _ _ _ _ _ _ _ _ _ _

Definition

Sentence

4. **per** (parts) + **cent** (hundred) = _ _ _ _ _ _ _

Definition

Sentence

20

cert certain, sure

certain- being **sure**
- They were **certain** that they saw the mountain lion!

uncert**ain** (**un-** *not*)- not being **certain** or **sure**
- We are **uncertain** about our vacation plans.

certify (**fy-** *to make*)- to make **sure**, **certain**, something is true
and correct
- The apples are **certified** organic.

certificate- an official document to insure **certain** facts are true.
- Why is your birth **certificate** an important document.

- Say each word.   - Underline the word roots.   - Write each word again as one word.

cert ain   **un cert** ain   **cert** i **fy**   **cert** ificate

---

- Write the complete word.   - Write the definition.   - Write the word in a sentence.

1. **cert** (sure) + ain = _ _ _ _ _ _ _

Definition

Sentence

2. **un** (not) + **cert** (sure) + ain = _ _ _ _ _ _ _ _ _

Definition

Sentence

3. **cert** (sure) + i + **fy** (make) = _ _ _ _ _ _ _

Definition

Sentence

4. **cert** (sure) + ificate = _ _ _ _ _ _ _ _ _ _ _

Definition

Sentence

chron time

chronic- lasting a long **time**, as in a disease or a disorder
- Is arthritis a **chronic** illness?

chronology (ology- *science of*)- the **science** of arranging events by **time**
- I made a **chronology** of the events in the Civil War.

syn**chron**ize (**syn-** *together, same*)- to happen at the same **time**
- The divers **synchronized** their watches before going into the water.

chronometer (**meter-** *to measure*)- an instrument that **measures** extremely accurate **time**
- How did the **chronometer** change navigation?

- Say each word.   - Underline the word roots.   - Write each word again as one word.

chron ic   **chron ology**   **syn chron** ize   **chron** o**meter**

- Write the complete word.   - Write the definition.   - Write the word in a sentence

1. **chron** (time) + ic = _ _ _ _ _ _ _

Definition

Sentence

2. **chron** (time) + **ology** (science of) = _ _ _ _ _ _ _ _ _ _

Definition

Sentence

3. **syn** (same) + **chron** (time) + ize =_ _ _ _ _ _ _ _ _ _ _

Definition

Sentence

4. **chron** (time) + o + **meter** (to measure) = _ _ _ _ _ _ _ _ _ _ _

Definition

Sentence

circ, circum

around

<u>circ</u>le (**circ-** *around*)- a **round** shape.
- We sat in a **circle around** the campfire.

<u>circ</u>us- a **circular** arena with seats all **around**; has clowns, etc.
- Have you been to a **circus**?

<u>circum</u>vent (**vent-** *to go*)- to bypass or **to go around**
- They must **circumvent** the obstacles in the mountain pass to get home.

<u>circum</u>navigate (**nav-** *sail*)- to **sail** or fly completely **around** something
- The ship will **circumnavigate** the globe.

- Say each word.   - Underline the word roots.   - Write each word again as one word.

circ le   **circ** us   **circum vent**   **circum nav** i gate

---

- Write the complete word.   - Write the definition.   - Write the word in a sentence.

1. **circ** (around) **+** le **=** _ _ _ _ _ _

Definition

Sentence

2. **circ** (around) **+** us **=** _ _ _ _ _ _

Definition

Sentence

3. **circum** (around) **+ vent** (to *go*) **=** _ _ _ _ _ _ _ _ _ _

Definition

Sentence

4. circum(around) **+ nav** (sail) **+**igate **=** _ _ _ _ _ _ _ _ _ _ _ _ _ _

Definition

Sentence

con, com
with, together

<u>con</u>nect- to link **together**
- **Connect** the hose to the faucet.

<u>con</u>greg**ate** (**greg**- *flock*)- to flock **together**; come **together**
- The pigeons **congregated** in the park.

<u>com</u>bine- put or add **together**
- **Combine** all of the ingredients to make a cake.

<u>com</u>muni**ty**- (**uni**- *one*)- a group of people that live **together** as **one** in the same place.
- Our **community** is building a new playground.

- -

- Say each word. • Underline the word roots. • Write each word again as one word.

con nect   **con greg** ate   **com** bine   **com** muni**t**y

---

- Write the complete word. • Write the definition. • Write the word in a sentence.

1. **con** (together) **+** nect = _ _ _ _ _ _ _

Definition

Sentence

2. **con** (together) **+ greg** (flock) **+** ate = _ _ _ _ _ _ _ _ _ _

Definition

Sentence

3. **com** (together) **+** bine =_ _ _ _ _ _ _

Definition

Sentence

4. **com** (together) **+** m **+uni** (one) **+** ty = _ _ _ _ _ _ _ _ _

Definition

Sentence

cycl/e circle, wheel

cycle- related events happening in the **same order**
- Spring, summer, autumn, and winter are the **cycle** of the four seasons.

recycle (re- *again***)-** to treat something so that it can be used **again**
- Put the newspapers in the **recycling** bin.

bicycle (bi- *two***)-** a **two-wheeled** vehicle that is ridden by pushing pedals
- The wheels on a bi**cycle** are like **circles**.

cyclone- a powerful wind moving in a **circle** around a calm central area
- The **cyclone** did much damage to the area.

- Say each word. • Underline the word roots. • Write each word again as one word.

cycle   **re cycle**   **bi cycle**   **cyclone**

- Write the complete word. • Write the definition. • Write the word in a sentence.

1. **cycle** (circle) = _ _ _ _ _

Definition

Sentence

2. **re** (again) **cycle** (circle) = _ _ _ _ _ _ _

Definition

Sentence

3. **bi** (two) + **cycle** (wheel) = _ _ _ _ _ _ _

Definition

Sentence

4. **cycl** (circle) + one = _ _ _ _ _ _ _

Definition

Sentence

25

dec ten

decade (**ad-** *group*)- a period of **ten** years; a **group** or series of ten
- The 1960s was an interesting **decade**.

decathlon (**athlon-** *contest*)- an athletic **contest** with **ten** events
- She is training for the Olympic **Decathlon**.

decimal- a number system based on **ten**
- In the United States, money is based on the **decimal** system.

decapod (**pod-** *foot*)- a **ten**-**footed** creature such as a crab or a shrimp.
- Why are lobsters called **decapods?**

- Say each word.   - Underline the word roots.   - Write each word again as one word.

dec ade   **dec athlon**   **dec** i mal   **dec** a **pod**

- Write the complete word.   - Write the definition.   - Write the word in a sentence.

1. dec (ten) **+ ad**e = _ _ _ _ _ _

Definition

Sentence

2. dec (ten) + athlon (contest) = _ _ _ _ _ _ _ _ _

Definition

Sentence

3. dec (ten) **+** imal **=** _ _ _ _ _ _ _

Definition

Sentence

4. dec (ten) **+** a **+ pod** (feet) **=** _ _ _ _ _ _ _

Definition

Sentence

GREEK

dem/o the people

<u>dem</u>ocracy (**cracy-** *government*)- a **government** run by the **people**
● Greeks were the first society with a **democracy**.
<u>dem</u>ocrat*ic* (**crat-** *government*) (**ic-** *having to do with*)- having to do with a **democracy**; a **democratic government**
● The United States is a **democratic** country.
epi<u>dem</u>ic (**epi-** *among*)- a rapidly spreading disease **among**
people in an area.
● Without vaccinations, there will be an **epidemic**.
pan<u>dem</u>ic (**pan-** *all*)- a rapidly spreading disease over **all**
or most **people**.
● Is a **pandemic** worse than an **epidemic**?

- - - - - - - - - - - - - - - - -

● Say each word.   ● Underline the word roots.   ● Write each word again as one word.

democracy   demo crat ic   epi dem ic   pan dem ic

● Write the complete word.   ● Write the definition.   ● Write the word in a sentence.

1.   **demo** (the people) **+ cracy** (government) = _ _ _ _ _ _ _ _ _

<u>Definition</u>

<u>Sentence</u>

2.   **demo** (the people) **crat** (government) **+ ic** = _ _ _ _ _ _ _ _ _ _

<u>Definition</u>

<u>Sentence</u>

3. **epi** (among) **+ dem** (people) **+ ic** = _ _ _ _ _ _ _ _

<u>Definition</u>

<u>Sentence</u>

4.   **pan** (all) **+ dem** (people) **+ ic** = _ _ _ _ _ _ _ _

<u>Definition</u>

<u>Sentence</u>

dict speak, say

dictate- **speak**; to command
● Did the teacher **dictate** the spelling words?
dictator (**or-** *one who*)- **one who speaks** with full authority; ruler of a country.
● Do some countries have **dictators**?
pre**dict** (**pre-** *before*)- to **say** what will happen **beforehand**
● Can you **predict** tomorrow's weather?
contra**dict** (**contra-** *against*)- to **say** or **speak against**
● I did not **contradict** her.

● Say each word.   ● Underline the word roots.   ● Write each word again as one word.

dictate   **dict**ator   **pre dict**   **contra dict**

● Write the complete word.   ● Write the definition.   ● Write the word in a sentence.

1. **dict** (speak, say) **+** ate **=** _ _ _ _ _ _ _

Definition

Sentence

2. **dict** (speak, say) **+** at **+ or** (one who) **=** _ _ _ _ _ _ _ _

Definition

Sentence

3. **pre** (before) **+ dict** (speak, say) **=** _ _ _ _ _ _ _

Definition

Sentence

4. **contra** (against) **+ dict** (speak, say) **=** _ _ _ _ _ _ _ _ _ _

Definition

Sentence

equ equal, same

<u>equ</u>al- exactly the **same**
- Four quarts are **equal** to one gallon.

<u>unequ</u>al (**un**- *not*)- **not** the same; not **equal**
- The sides are **unequal.**

<u>equ</u>ality- being **equal**
- We believe in the **equality** of all people.

<u>equ</u>ilateral (**lat**- *side*)- having all **sides equal**
- All three sides of an **equilateral** triangle are the same.

- Say each word.   • Underline the word roots.   • Write each word again as one word.

equal   **un equ**al   **equ**al ity   **equi lat** eral

- Write the complete word.   • Write the definition.   • Write the word in a sentence.

1. **equ** (*equal, same*) **+** al **=** _ _ _ _ _

Definition

Sentence

2. **un** (*not*) **+ equ** (*equal, same*) **+** al **=** _ _ _ _ _ _ _

Definition

Sentence

3. **equ** (*equal, same*) **+** ality **=** _ _ _ _ _ _ _ _

Definition

Sentence

4. **equ** (*equal, same*) **+** i **+ lat** (*side*) **+** eral **=** _ _ _ _ _ _ _ _ _ _

Definition

Sentence

ex out, from

<u>ex</u>it- a way to go **out**

<u>ex</u>pel- (**pel**- *drive*) to **drive** or throw **out**
- They were **expelled** from school.

<u>ex</u>tend (**ten**d- *stretch*)- to **stretch out**
- We will **extend** our vacation by three days.

<u>ex</u>claim (**claim**- *cry out*)- to cry **out**; to shout **out**
- "We won the game!" he **exclaimed**.

- Say each word. • Underline the word roots. • Write each word again as one word.

ex it   **ex pel**   **ex tend**   **ex claim**

• Write the complete word. • Write the definition. • Write the word in a sentence.

1. **ex** (out) **+** it **=** _ _ _ _

Definition _____

Sentence _____

2. **ex** (out) **+ pel** (throw) **=** _ _ _ _ _

Definition _____

Sentence _____

3. **ex** (out) **+ tend** (stretch) **=** _ _ _ _ _ _

Definition _____

Sentence _____

4. **ex** (out) **+ claim** (cry out) **=** _ _ _ _ _ _ _

Definition _____

Sentence _____

fin finish, end, limit

finish- to complete or reach the **end**; conclusion
● Did you **finish** your homework?
in**fin**ite (**in-** *not*)- **not** having an **end**; exceedingly great
● An **infinite** number of possibilities is without **end; limitless**.
de**fin**e- to **limit**; to give the meaning of a word or idea
● The dictionary gives **definitions** for; **defines** words.
con**fin**e- (**con-** *together*) to put within **limits**; to keep **together** in a small space.
● Zoo animals are **confined**.

● Say each word.　● Underline the word roots.　● Write each word again as one word.

fin ish　　　　**in fin** ite　　　　de **fine**　　　　**con** fine

● Write the complete word.　● Write the definition.　● Write the word in a sentence.

1.　**fin** (finish, end) **+** ish **=** _ _ _ _ _ _

Definition

Sentence

2.　**in** (not) **+ fin** (end) + ite **=** _ _ _ _ _ _ _ _

Definition

Sentence

3. de **+ fin** (limit) **+** e **=** _ _ _ _ _ _

Definition

Sentence

4.　**con** (together) **+ fin** (limit) + e **=** _ _ _ _ _ _ _

Definition

Sentence

flor flower

<u>flor</u>a- **flowers** and other plant life of a particular place or time
- The desert **flora** are beautiful this time of year.

<u>flor</u>ist (ist- *one who*)- **one who** grows and sells **flowers**
- The local **florist** buys and sells flowers.

<u>Flor</u>ida- a state whose name means *land of the* **flowers**
- Florida has many beautiful **flowers**.

<u>flor</u>icult**ure** (**cult**- *cultivate*)- the **cultivation** (preparing the land) to grow flowers
- **Floriculture** is an important industry

- Say each word.   - Underline the word roots.   - Write each word again as one word.

flor a   **flor ist**   **Flor** i da   **flor** i **cult**ure

---

- Write the complete word.   - Write the definition.   - Write the word in a sentence.

1. **flor** (flowers) **+** a **=** _ _ _ _ _

<u>Definition</u>

<u>Sentence</u>

2. **flor** (flowers) **+ ist** (one who) **=** _ _ _ _ _ _ _ _

<u>Definition</u>

<u>Sentence</u>

3. **Flor** (flower) **+** ida **=** _ _ _ _ _ _ _

<u>Definition</u>

<u>Sentence</u>

4. **flor** (flower) **+ i + cult** (cultivate) **+ ure =** _ _ _ _ _ _ _ _ _ _ _ _

<u>Definition</u>

<u>Sentence</u>

graph write, draw

bio<u>graph</u>y (**bio-** *life*)- the true story of one's **life written** by another person

● My favorite stories are **biographies** of people's lives.

autobio<u>graph</u>y (**auto-** *self*)- the true story of one's life **written** by that person. ● Someday I will write my **autobiography**.

auto<u>**graph**</u> (**auto-** *self*)- signature **written** by one's **self.**

● I have an **autograph** from my favorite baseball player.

biblio<u>**graph**</u>y (**biblio-** *book*)- a list of **books** about a subject.

● This book about lions has a **bibliography** in the back.

● Say each word.   ● Underline the word roots.   ● Write each word again as one word.

biography   auto biography   auto graph   bibliography

● Write the complete word.   ● Write the definition.   ● Write the word in a sentence.

1. bio (life) **+ graph** (written) **+ y =** _ _ _ _ _ _ _ _ _
<u>**Definition**</u>

<u>**Sentence**</u>

2. auto(self) **+ bio**(life) **+ graph**(written) **+ y =**_ _ _ _ _ _ _ _ _ _ _ _ _
<u>**Definition**</u>

<u>**Sentence**</u>

3. auto (self) **+ graph** (write) **=** _ _ _ _ _ _ _ _ _
<u>**Definition**</u>

<u>**Sentence**</u>

4. biblio (book) **+ graph** (write) **+ y =** _ _ _ _ _ _ _ _ _ _ _ _
<u>**Definition**</u>

<u>**Sentence**</u>

hosp guest house

<u>hosp</u>ital- a **guest house**; a place that cares for the sick
- I am going to visit my friend in the **hospital**.

<u>hosp</u>itality- **able to** treat **guests** in a friendly way
- We thanked our friends for their **hospitality**.

host stranger, enemy

<u>host</u>age- a person who is held prisoner by a **stranger** or **enemy** until money is paid or promises kept
- The **hostages** were held until a ransom was paid.

<u>host</u>el- a place that gives low priced lodging to **strangers**.
- Bike riders and hikers like to stay in youth **hostels**.

- Say each word.   - Underline the word roots.   - Write each word again as one word.

hosp ital   **hosp** tality   **host** age   **host** el

- Write the complete word.   - Write the definition.   - Write the word in a sentence.

1. **hosp** (guest house) + ital = _ _ _ _ _ _ _ _

Definition

Sentence

2. **hosp** (guest house) + itality + = _ _ _ _ _ _ _ _ _ _ _

Definition

Sentence

3. **host** (stranger, enemy) + age = _ _ _ _ _ _ _ _

Definition

Sentence

4. **host** (stranger) + el = _ _ _ _ _ _

Definition

Sentence

logy/ology

study of, science of

biology (bio- *life*)- the **study of life** ●Who is your **biology** teacher?.
chronology- *(chron- time)*- the **science of** arranging events according to **time**

●The chart showed a **chronology** of American inventions.
ecology- (eco- *environment*)- the **scientific study of** plants, animals and people to their **environments**

●My class project is about **ecology** and saving our planet.
zoology (zo- *animal*)- the **study of animals**

● **Zoology** is a branch of biology.

●Say each word.   ●Underline the word roots.   ●Write each word again as one word.

biology   **chron ology**   **ecology**   **zo ology**

● Write the complete word. ● Write the definition.   ●Write the word in a sentence.

1.   bio (life) + **logy** (study of) = _ _ _ _ _ _ _

Definition

Sentence

2. chron (time) + **ology** (science of) = _ _ _ _ _ _ _ _ _ _

Definition

Sentence

3. eco (environment) + **ology** (science of) = _ _ _ _ _ _ _ _

Definition

Sentence

4. zo (animal) **+ ology** (study of) = _ _ _ _ _ _ _ _

Definition

Sentence

35

medi middle

medial, median- situated at or near the middle
- In a series of numbers, the median is the middle number.

intermediate (inter- *between*)- in the middle; being between
- The school has beginning, intermediate, and advanced math classes.

Medieval- belonging to the Middle Ages
- We are learning about the children in Medieval society.

mediterranean (terr- *land*)- the middle land
- The Mediterranean is a great inland sea between Europe, Asia, and Africa.

- Say each word.   - Underline the word roots.   - Write each word again as one word.

median   inter mediate   Medi eval   medi terr anean

- Write the complete word.   - Write the definition.   - Write the word in a sentence.

1. medi (middle) + an = _ _ _ _ _ _
Definition

Sentence

2. inter (between) **+ medi** (middle) **+ ate =** _ _ _ _ _ _ _ _ _ _ _ _
Definition

Sentence

3. Medi (middle) **+ eval =** _ _ _ _ _ _ _ _
Definition

Sentence

4. medi (middle) **+ terr** (land) **+ anian=** _ _ _ _ _ _ _ _ _ _ _ _ _
Definition

Sentence

GREEK

nov new

<u>nov</u>el- a **new**, original idea   ●I have a **novel** idea to save energy.
<u>nov</u>ice- a beginner, a **new** trainee, an apprentice

●I am a **novice** swimmer; I have had little experience.
in<u>nov</u>ation (**in**- *in, into*)- the **in**troduction of something **new**

●There have been many **innovations** in the computer industry.
re<u>nov</u>ate (**re**- *again*)- to make **new again**

●They are going to **renovate** the old shopping center.

●Say each word.   ●Underline the word roots.   ●Write each word again as one word.

nov el   **nov** ice   **in nov**ation   **renov**ate

● Write the complete word.   ● Write the definition.   ●Write the word in a sentence.

1. **nov** (new) **+** el **=** _ _ _ _ _

<u>Definition</u>

<u>Sentence</u>

2. **nov** (new) **+** ice **=** _ _ _ _ _ _

<u>Definition</u>

<u>Sentence</u>

3. **in** (in, into) **+ nov** (new) **+** ation **=** _ _ _ _ _ _ _ _ _ _

<u>Definition</u>

<u>Sentence</u>

4. **re** (again) **+ nov** (new) **+** ate **=** _ _ _ _ _ _ _ _

<u>Definition</u>

<u>Sentence</u>

GREEK

nym, onym name, word

synonym (syn- *same)-* a **word** with the **same** or similar meaning as another word ●The words *happy* and *glad* are **synonyms.**
antonym (ant- *opposite)-* a **word** that has the **opposite** meaning of another word ●The words *fast* and *slow* are **antonyms.**
homonym (homo- *same)-* a **word** that sounds the **same** as another **word** but has a different spelling and meaning
●The words *feet* and *feat* are **homonyms.**
anonymous **(an-** *without)-* **without** a **name**
●The gift was from an **anonymous** donor.

●Say each word.   ●Underline the word roots.   ●Write each word again as one word.

syn onym   **ant onym**   **hom onym**   **an onym**ous

● Write the complete word.   ● Write the definition.   ●Write the word in a sentence.

1.   syn (same) + onym (word) = _ _ _ _ _ _ _ _

Definition

Sentence

2. ant (opposite) + onym (word) = _ _ _ _ _ _ _ _

Definition

Sentence

3. homo (same) + nym (word) = _ _ _ _ _ _ _ _

Definition

Sentence

4. an (without) + onym (name) + ous **=** _ _ _ _ _ _ _ _ _ _

Definition

Sentence

38

omni all

omnipoten**t** (poten- *powerful*)- **all powerful**; having unlimited authority ●The **omnipotent** ruler is a kind man.
omnivore (vor- *to eat*)- **eating all** things, meat and plants
 ●Bears are **omnivores.**

pan all

panacea (cea- **cure**)- a presumed **cure** for **all** evils, ills, and difficulties ●The new diet was a **panacea** for losing weight.
panorama (orama- *view*)- a complete or wide view of an area, to see **all** of an area.
 ●You can see a **panorama** of the valley from the mountaintop.

●Say each word.　●Underline the word roots.　●Write each word again as one word.

omni potent　　**omni vor**e　　**pan** a **cea**　　**pan orama**

● Write the complete word.　● Write the definition.　●Write the word in a sentence.

1.　omni (all) **+ poten** (powerful) + t **=** _ _ _ _ _ _ _ _ _ _

Definition _____

Sentence _____

2.　omni (all) **+ vor** (to eat) **=** _ _ _ _ _ _ _ _

Definition _____

Sentence _____

3.　pan (all) **+** a **+ cea** (cure) **=** _ _ _ _ _ _ _

Definition _____

Sentence _____

4.　pan (all) **+ orama** (view) **=** _ _ _ _ _ _ _ _

Definition _____

Sentence _____

ped foot, feet

pedal- **foot** operated lever ● She **pedaled** her bike across town.

pedestrian- one traveling on **foot,** especially on a street used by cars ● That street is not safe for **pedestrians**.

bi**ped** (**bi**- *two*)- two footed animal; a person walking on two feet ● Are you a **biped** or a **quadruped**?

pedicure (**cure**- *care*)- **care** and treatment of the **feet**

● Have you had a **pedicure**?

● Say each word.   ● Underline the word roots.   ● Write each word again as one word.

ped al   ped estrian   bi ped   ped i cure

● Write the complete word.   ● Write the definition.   ● Write the word in a sentence.

1.   ped (foot) + al **=** _ _ _ _ _

<u>Definition</u>

<u>Sentence</u>

2. ped (foot) + estrian **=** _ _ _ _ _ _ _ _ _ _

<u>Definition</u>

<u>Sentence</u>

3. bi (two) + ped (feet) = _ _ _ _ _

<u>Definition</u>

<u>Sentence</u>

4. ped (feet) + i **cure (care) =** _ _ _ _ _ _ _ _ _

<u>Definition</u>

<u>Sentence</u>

pri, prim, first

primary (ary- *relating to*)- **relating to first** in order of time
- Grades one, two, and three are the **primary** grades

primitive- **first**, from the earliest times -a **primitive** culture
- A stone ax is a **primitive** tool.

primate- **first** in rank, the order of mammals; man, monkey, etc. - All **primates** have large brains.

priority (ity- *state of*)- **state of** being **first**; most important
- My **first priority** is completing my homework.

- Say each word. - Underline the word roots. - Write each word again as one word.

pri mary   **prim** i tive   **pri** mate   **pri** or **ity**

- Write the complete word. - Write the definition. - Write the word in a sentence.

1. prim (first) + ary (relating to) = _ _ _ _ _ _ _
Definition _____

Sentence _____

2. prim (first) + itive = _ _ _ _ _ _ _ _ _
Definition _____

Sentence _____

3. pri (first) + mate = _ _ _ _ _ _ _
Definition _____

Sentence _____

4. pri (first) + or + ity (state of) = _ _ _ _ _ _ _ _
Definition _____

Sentence _____

tend, tens stretch, strain

extend (**ex-** *out*)- **stretch** out; continue
- The bank will **extend** my credit for four more years

tense- **strained**; anxious -a **tense** moment
- He was so **tense**, his neck ached.

intensity- **strain**; force - The **intensity** of the wind is increasing.
hypertension (**hyper-** *above, over*)- **overly strained**; high blood pressure - Exercise helps to lower **hypertension**.

- Say each word.   - Underline the word roots.   - Write each word again as one word.

ex tend   **tens**e   in **tens ity**   **hyper tens**ion

- Write the complete word.   - Write the definition.   - Write the word in a sentence.

1. **ex** (out) **+ tend** (stretch out) = _ _ _ _ _ _

Definition

Sentence

2. **tens** (strained) **+** e = _ _ _ _ _

Definition

Sentence

3. in **+ tens** (strain) **+ ity** = _ _ _ _ _ _ _ _ _

Definition

Sentence

4. **hyper** (above, over) **+ tens** (strain) **+** ion = _ _ _ _ _ _ _ _ _ _ _ _

Definition

Sentence

terr land

LATIN

terrace- a level area of **land** next to a house; an outdoor living area; the balcony of an apartment
- They enjoy relaxing on the **terrace**.

territory- a large tract of **land**; a region
- Hawaii was a **territory** until it became a United States state in 1959.

me**diterr**anean (**medi-** *middle*)- in the **middle**; almost completely surrounded by dry **land**
- Can you locate the **Mediterranean** Sea on the map?

terrarium (**arium-** *a place for*)- **a place for** growing small plants or raising small animals. - She put the baby turtles in a **terrarium**.

- Say each word.   • Underline the word roots.   • Write each word again as one word.

terrace   **terr** i tory   **medi terr** anean   **terr arium**

- Write the complete word.   • Write the definition.   • Write the word in a sentence.

1.   terr (land) + ace **=** _ _ _ _ _ _ _

Definition

Sentence

2. terr (land) + itory **=** _ _ _ _ _ _ _ _ _

Definition

Sentence

3. medi (middle) + terr (land) + anean **=** _ _ _ _ _ _ _ _ _ _ _ _ _

Definition

Sentence

4. terr (land) **+ arium** (a place for) **=** _ _ _ _ _ _ _ _ _ _

Definition

Sentence

43

tract draw, pull

tractor- a farm vehicle used to **pull** heavy equipment
- Years ago the **tractor** replaced the horse on the farm.

attract (**at**- *to*)- **to draw** in; to **pull** toward; to notice
- Flowers **attract** bees.

distract (**dis**- *away*)- to **draw** attention **away**
- A loud noise **distracted** me.

extract (**ex**- *out*) to **draw out**; to remove
- The dentist will **extract** the decayed tooth.

- Say each word. • Underline the word roots. • Write each word again as one word.

tract or   **at tract**   **dis tract**   **ex tract**

- Write the complete word. • Write the definition. • Write the word in a sentence.

1. **tract** (pull) **+ or =** _ _ _ _ _ _ _

Definition

Sentence

2. **at** (to) **+ tract** (draw, pull) **=** _ _ _ _ _ _ _

Definition

Sentence

3. **dis** (away) **+ tract** (draw, pull) **=** _ _ _ _ _ _ _ _ _

Definition

Sentence

4. **ex** (out) **+ tract** (draw, pull) **=** _ _ _ _ _ _ _ _

Definition

Sentence

uni one

<u>uni</u>ted- together as **one** ● America is made of fifty **united** states.
<u>uni</u>form- always the same; not changing
  ●The school band has new **uniforms**.
<u>uni</u>cycle (**cycl-** *wheel*)- a type of bicycle with only **one wheel**.
  ●The clown rides a **unicycle** at the circus.
<u>uni</u>son (**son-** *sound*)- making the same **sounds** or movements at the same time. ●The choir sang in **unison**.

●Say each word.   ●Underline the word roots.   ●Write each word again as one word.

<u>uni</u>ted   **uni** form   **uni cycle**   **uni son**

● Write the complete word.   ● Write the definition.   ●Write the word in a sentence.

1. uni (one) + ted **=** _ _ _ _ _ _
<u>Definition</u>

<u>Sentence</u>

2. uni (one) + form **=** _ _ _ _ _ _ _
<u>Definition</u>

<u>Sentence</u>

3. uni (one) + cycl (wheel) + e **=** _ _ _ _ _ _ _ _
<u>Definition</u>

<u>Sentence</u>

4. uni (one) **+ son** (sound) **=** _ _ _ _ _ _
<u>Definition</u>

<u>Sentence</u>

45

vis, vid see

vision- the ability to **see**; eyesight ● I have excellent **vision**.

visible (ible- *able to*)- **able to** be **seen**

● The stars are not **visible** tonight.

in**vis**ible (in- *not*)- **not** able to be **seen**

● The stars are **invisible** tonight.

video- picture part, or what is **seen**, on television

● The bank has a **video** camera for security.

● Say each word.　● Underline the word roots.　● Write each word again as one word.

vision　　　　**vis ible**　　　　　**in vis ible**　　　　**vid** eo

● Write the complete word.　● Write the definition.　● Write the word in a sentence.

1.　vis (see) + ion = _ _ _ _ _ _

Definition

Sentence

2. vis (see) **+ ible** (able to) = _ _ _ _ _ _ _

Definition

Sentence

3. in (not) + vis (see) + ible (able to) = _ _ _ _ _ _ _ _ _

Definition

Sentence

4. vid (see) + eo = _ _ _ _ _

Definition

Sentence

PART 1

LESSON ANSWERS

Lesson, Answers

(Except for the word roots, the lesson answers are given. The lesson word roots are listed below.)

LESSON 1: act   **in act** ive   **re act**   **inter act**

LESSON 2: **anim**al   **anim**ate   **in anim**ate   **magn**animous

LESSON 3: **aqua** tic   **aqu arium**   **aqu** e **duct**   **aqua naut**

LESSON 4: **hydr**ant **de hydr** ate   **hydr** o **phobia**   **hydr** o electric

LESSON 5: **art**   **art ist**   **art**isan   **art** i **fic** ial

LESSON 6: **aud ible in aud ible aud**ience   **aud**ition

LESSON 7: **bi cycl**e **bi lingu** al   **bio logy**   **bio graph** y

LESSON 8: ac**cept**   **inter cept**   **cap able**   **cap**ture

LESSON 9: **cent**ury   **cent enn** ial **bi cent enn** ial   **per cent**

LESSON 10: **cert**ain **un cert**ain   **cert** i **fy**   **cert** ificate

LESSON 11: **chron**ic   **chron ology**   **syn chron** ize   **chron** o **meter**

LESSON 12: **circ**le   **circ**us   **circ** um **vent circ** um **nav** igate

LESSON 13: **con**nect   **con greg** ate **com**bine   **com** m **uni** ty

LESSON 14: **cycl**e   **re cycl**e   **bi cycl**e   **cycl** one

LESSON 15   **dec ad**e   **dec athlon**   **dec** imal   **dec** a **pod**

LESSON 16: **demo cracy**   **demo crat** ic   **epi dem** ic   **pan dem** ic

LESSON 17: **dict** ate   **dict** at **or**   **pre dict**   **contra dict**

Lesson Answers, Continued

LESSON 18: **equ**al   **un equal**   **equ**ality   **equi lat** eral

LESSON 19: **exit**   **ex pel**   **ex tend**   **ex claim**

LESSON 20: **fini**sh   **in fin** ite   de **fin**e   **con fin**e

LESSON 21: **flor**a   **flor ist**   **Flor**ida   **flor** i **cult** ure

LESSON 22: **bio graph** y   **auto bio graph** y   **auto graph**   **biblio graph** y

LESSON 23: **hosp**ital   **hosp** ital **ity**   **host**age   **host**el

LESSON 24: **bio logy** _   **chron ology**   **eco logy**   **zo ology**

LESSON 25: **medi** an   **inter medi** ate   **Medi_** eval   **medi terr** anean

LESSON 26: **nov**el   **nov**ice   **in nov** ation   **re nov** ate

LESSON 27: **syn onym ant onym**   **homo nym**   **an onym**ous_

LESSON 28: omni **poten**t   **omni vor**e   **pan** a cea   **pan orama**

LESSON 29: **ped**al   **ped** estrian__   **bi ped**   **ped** i **cure**

LESSON 30: **prim ary** primitive   **pri**mate   **pri** or **ity**

LESSON 31: **ex tend**   **tens**e   **in tens** ity   **hyper tens** ion

LESSON 32: **terr** ace   **terr** itory   **med**i **terr** anean   **terr arium**

LESSON 33: **tractor**   **at tract**   **dis tract**   **ex tract**

LESSON 34: **uni** ted   **un**i form   **uni cycl** e   **uni** son

LESSON 35: **vis** ion   **vis ible**   **in vis ible**   **vid**eo

PART 2

LESSON TESTS

(TEST 1 ACT)   act   react   inactive   interact

● Draw an arc under each word root. ● Write the word for each definition.

1. _____ to act between and together with others

2. _____ not active; not doing anything

3. _____ to act again; to respond to

4. _____ to do something

● Write the meanings for the word roots.

not	to do	again	between

5. re_____   6. act_____   7. inter_____   8. in_____

- -

(TEST 2 ANIM) animal   animate   magnanimous   inanimate

● Draw an arc under each word root. ● Write the word for each definition.

1. _____ to make alive; lively; full of life and spirit

2. _____ a living thing

3. _____ great; generous spirit: forgiving

4. _____ without life or spirit

● Write the meanings for the word roots.

life, spirit	without	great

5. in_____   6. anim_____   7. magn_____

- -

(TEST 3 AQU, AQUA)   aquatic aquanaut   aqueduct aquarium

● Draw an arc under each word root. ● Write the word for each definition.

1. _____ a large pipe or canal

2. _____ things happening in or on the water

3. _____ a place for keeping fishes and marine plants

4. _____ an underwater explorer

● Write the meanings for the word roots.

water	to lead	a place for	explorer

5. duct_____   6. aqu_____   7. naut_____   8. arium_____

(TEST 4 HYDR) hydrophobia dehydrate hydroelectric hydrant

● Draw an arc under each word root. ● Write the word for each definition.

1. _____ a large water pipe for drawing water

2. _____ fear of water

3. _____ producing electricity by the action of falling water

4. _____ to remove all water from

● Write the meanings for the word roots.

fear	water	remove

5. **hydr**_____ 6. **phobia**_____ 7. **de**_____

(TEST 5 ART) artist artisan art artificial

● Draw an arc under each word root. ● Write the word for each definition.

1. _____ a skill by which one creates

2. _____ made by skilled people, not by nature

3. _____ one who is skilled in music and literature

4. _____ a person skilled in a particular craft; carpenter etc.

● Write the meanings for the word roots.

make	skill	one who

5. **fic**_____ 6. **art**_____ 7. **ist**_____

(TEST 6 AUD) audible inaudible audition audience

● Draw an arc under each word root. ● Write the word for each definition.

1. _____ not able to be heard

2. _____ able to be heard

3. _____ a hearing

4. _____ a group of listeners

● Write the meanings for the word roots.

able to	hear, listen	not

5. **aud**_____ 6. **ible**_____ 7. **in**_____

(TEST 7 BI, BIO)   bicycle   biology   biography   bilingual

- Draw an arc under each word root. ● Write the word for each definition.

1. _____ able to use two languages
2. _____ a light vehicle with two large wheels
3. _____ the study of life
4. _____ one's life story written by another

- Write the meanings for the word roots

| two | life | study | write | wheel | language |

5. bio_____   6. graph_____   7. logy_____

8. lingu_____   9. cycl_____   10. bi_____

(TEST 8 CAP, CEPT)   accept   intercept   capable   capture

- Draw an arc under each word root. ● Write the word for each definition.

1. _____ to come between; to take before

2. _____ to receive; to agree to

3. _____ to take charge of; control by force

4. _____ able to receive knowledge; clever

- Write the meanings for the word roots.

| between | able to | take, receive |

5. cept_____   6. inter_____   7. able _____

(TEST 9 CENT)   percent   century   centennial   bicentennial

- Draw an arc under each word root. ● Write the word for each definition.

1. _____ a period of 100 years

2. _____ happening once every 100 years

3. _____ happening once every 200 years

4. _____ number of parts per hundred

- Write the meanings for the word roots.

| years | part | hundred | two |

5. per_____   6. bi_____   7. cent_____   8. enn_____

(TEST 10 CERT) uncertain certain certificate certify

- Draw an arc under each word root. ● Write the word for each definition.

1. _____ being sure

2. _____ not being certain or sure

3. _____ to make sure, certain, something is true

4. _____ an official document

- Write the meanings for the word roots.

make	not	sure

5. cert_____ 6. un_____ 7. fy_____

(TEST 11 CHRON) chronic chronometer synchronize chronology

- Draw an arc under each word root. ● Write the word for each definition.

1. _____ to happen at the same time

2. _____ an instrument that measures time

3. _____ the science of arranging events according to time

4. _____ lasting a long time

- Write the meanings for the word roots.

time	measure	science of	together, same

5. ology_____ 6. chron_____ 7. meter_____ 8. syn_____

(TEST 12 CIRC, CIRCUM) circus circle circumvent circumnavigate

- Draw an arc under each word root. ● Write the word for each definition.

1. _____ to bypass or to go around

2. _____ a round shape

3. _____ a circular arena with seats

4. _____ to sail or fly completely around

- Write the meanings for the word roots.

sail	to go	around

5. circ_____ 6. vent_____ 7. nav_____

(TEST 13 CON, COM) combine   connect   community   congregate

● Draw an arc under each word root. ● Write the word for each definition.

1. _____ a group of people that live together

2. _____ to flock together

3. _____ put or add together; as in making a cake

4. _____ to link together

● Write the meanings for the word roots.

one	flock	with, together

5. **greg**_____   6. **con, com**_____   7. **uni**_____

(TEST 14 CYCL/E)   bicycle   recycle   cyclone   cycle

● Draw an arc under each word root. ● Write the word for each definition.

1. _____ events happening in the same order

2. _____ to treat something so that it can be used again

3. _____ a two-wheeled vehicle

4. _____ a powerful wind moving in a circle

● Write the meanings for the word roots.

again	two	circle

5. **bi**_____   6. **cycl**_____   7. **re**_____

(TEST 15 DEC)   decade   decapod   decathlon   decimal

● Draw an arc under each word root. ● Write the word for each definition.

1. _____ a period or group of ten years

2. _____ a number system based on ten

3. _____ a ten-footed creature such as a crab or shrimp

4. _____ an athletic contest with ten events

● Write the meanings for the word roots.

foot	ten	contest	group

5. **dec**_____   6. **athlon**_____   7. **pod**_____   8. **ad**_____

(TEST 16 DEM/O) democratic democracy pandemic epidemic

- Draw an arc under each word root. • Write the word for each definition.

1. _____ having to do with a democracy

2. _____ government run by the people

3. _____ a rapidly spreading disease all over

4. _____ a rapidly spreading disease in an area

- Write the meanings for the word roots.

government	all	among	the people

5. **cracy**_____ 6. **epi**_____ 7. **pan**_____ 8. **dem**_____

(TEST 17 DICT) contradict dictator dictate predict

- Draw an arc under each word root. • Write the word for each definition.

1. _____ one who speaks with full authority;

2. _____ to say what will happen beforehand

3. _____ to say or speak against

4. _____ to speak; to command

- Write the meanings for the word roots.

before	against	speak	one who

5. **contra**_____ 6. **dict**_____ 7. **or**_____ 8. **pre**_____

(TEST 18 EQU) equal unequal equilateral equality

- Draw an arc under each word root. • Write the word for each definition.

1. _____ exactly the same

2. _____ not the same; not equal

3. _____ all people being equal

4. _____ having all sides equal

- Write the meanings for the word roots.

side	equal, same	not

5. **lat**_____ 6. **un**_____ 7. **equ**_____

(TEST 19 EX)   extend   exclaim   expel   exit

- Draw an arc under each word root. ● Write the word for each definition.

1. _____ a way to go out

2. _____to drive or throw out

3. _____ to cry out

4. _____ to stretch out

- Write the meanings for the word roots.

| drive | out, from | cry out | stretch |

5. ex_____   6. tend_____   7. pel_____   8. claim_____

(TEST 20 FIN)   define   finish   confine   infinite

- Draw an arc under each word root. ● Write the word for each definition.

1. _____ not having an end; exceedingly great

2. _____to complete or reach the end; conclusion

3. _____ to keep together in a small space.

4. _____ to limit; to give the meaning of a word or idea

- Write the meanings for the word roots.

| finish, end, limit | not | together |

5. con_____   6. in_____   7. fin_____

(TEST 21 FLOR)   flora   florist   Florida   floriculture

- Draw an arc under each word root. ● Write the word for each definition.

1. _____ a state whose name means *land of the* flowers

2. _____one who grows and sells flowers

3. _____ flowers and other plant life

4. _____ the cultivation; preparing the land to grow flowers

- Write the meanings for the word roots.

| cultivate | one who | flower |

5. ist_____   6. cult_____   7. flor_____

(TEST 22 GRAPH)   bibliography   autobiography   biography   autograph

● Draw an arc under each word root. ● Write the word for each definition.

1. _____ signature written by one self

2. _____ the true story of one's life written by another person

3. _____ the true story of one's life written by that person

4. _____ a list of books about a subject

● Write the meanings for the word roots.

| self | life | write, draw | book |

5. bio_____ 6. graph_____ 7. biblio_____ 8. auto_____

- -

(TEST 23 HOSP, HOST)   hospital   hostage   hospitality   hostel

● Draw an arc under each word root. ● Write the word for each definition.

1. _____ a place that gives cheap shelter to strangers.

2. _____ able to treat guests in a friendly way

3. _____ a person who is held prisoner by a stranger

4. _____ a guest house; a place that cares for the sick

● Write the meanings for the word roots.

| stranger, enemy | guest house |

5. host_____ 6. hosp_____

- -

(TEST 24 LOGY/OLOGY)   zoology   biology   ecology   chronology

● Draw an arc under each word root. ● Write the word for each definition.

1. _____ the study of life

2. _____ the scientific study of animals

3. _____ study of animals and people in their environments

4. _____ the science of arranging events according to time

● Write the meanings for the word roots.

| environment | time | animal | study of, science of |

5. chron _____ 6. eco_____ 7. zo_____ 8. ology _____

(TEST 25 MEDI) **Medieval**   **median**   **intermediate**   **Mediterranean**

● Draw an arc under each word root. ● Write the word for each definition.

1. _____ belonging to the Middle Ages.

2. _____ situated at or near the middle

3. _____ the middle land

4. _____ in the middle; being between

● Write the meanings for the word roots.

middle	between	land

5. **inter** _____   6. **medi** _____   7. **terr** _____

(TEST 26 NOV)   **novice**   **renovate**   **novel**   **innovation**

● Draw an arc under each word root. ● Write the word for each definition.

1. _____ a beginner, a new trainee, an apprentice

2. _____ a new, original idea

3. _____ to make new again

4. _____ the introduction of something new

● Write the meanings for the word roots.

into	new	again

5. **in** _____   6. **nov** _____   7. **re** _____

(TEST 27 NYM, ONYM) **homonym** **synonym** **antonym** **anonymous**

● Draw an arc under each word root. ● Write the word for each definition.

1. _____ without a name

2. _____ a word with similar meaning as another word

3. _____ a word with the opposite meaning of another word

4. _____ a word that sounds the same as another word but has a different spelling and meaning

● Write the meanings for the word roots.

opposite	same	without	name, word

5. **syn, homo** _____   6. **nym, onym** _____   7. **ant** _____   8. **an** _____

(TEST 28 OMNI, PAN) omnipotent omnivore panorama panacea

- Draw an arc under each word root. ● Write the word for each definition.

1. _____ a complete or wide view to see all of an area

2. _____ all powerful; having unlimited authority

3. _____ a presumed cure for all evils, ills, and difficulties

4. _____ eating all things, meat and plants

- Write the meanings for the word roots.

all	to eat	cure	view	powerful

5. omni, pan _____ 6. vor_____ 7. orama_____ 8. cea_____ 9. poten____

━━━━━━━━━━━━━━━━━━━━━━━━━━━━━━━━━━━━━━━

(TEST 29 PED)   biped   pedal   pedicure   pedestrian

- Draw an arc under each word root. ● Write the word for each definition.

1. _____ foot operated lever

2. _____ one traveling on foot, especially on a street

3. _____ two footed animal

4. _____ care and treatment of the feet

- Write the meanings for the word roots.

foot, feet	two	care

5. bi _____ 6. ped_____ 7. cure_____

━━━━━━━━━━━━━━━━━━━━━━━━━━━━━━━━━━━━━━━

(TEST 30 PRI, PRIM) primitive priority primate primary

- Draw an arc under each word root. ● Write the word for each definition.

1. _____ first, from the earliest times: a _____ culture

2. _____ first in rank, the order of mammals; from human etc.

3. _____ state of being first; most important

4. _____ relating to first in order of time; the_____grades

- Write the meanings for the word roots.

state of	first	relating to

5. ary _____ 6. ity_____ 7. pri, prim_____

(TEST 31 TEND, TENS)   intensity   extend   tense   hypertension

● Draw an arc under each word root. ● Write the word for each definition.

1. _____ strained; anxious

2. _____ stretch out; continue

3. _____ overly strained; high blood pressure

4. _____ strain; force; the _____ of the wind

● Write the meanings for the word roots.

above, over	out	stretch, strain

5. ex _____   6. hyper _____   7. tend, tens _____

- -

(TEST 32 TERR)   territory   terrarium   terrace   mediterranean

● Draw an arc under each word root. ● Write the word for each definition.

1. _____ an outdoor living area; the balcony of an apartment

2. _____ a large tract of land; a region

3. _____ almost completely surrounded by dry land

4. _____ a place for growing small plants and animals

● Write the meanings for the word roots.

middle	a place for	land

5. terr _____   6. medi _____   7. arium _____

- -

(TEST 33 TRACT)   extract   tractor   attract   distract

● Draw an arc under each word root. ● Write the word for each definition.

1. _____ a farm vehicle used to **pull** heavy equipment

2. _____ **to draw** in; to **pull** toward; to notice

3. _____ to **draw out**; to remove

4. _____ to **draw** attention **away**

● Write the meanings for the word roots.

out	away	draw, pull	to

5. ex _____   6. at _____   7. dis _____   8. tract _____

61

(TEST 34 UNI)   unison   unicycle   uniform   united

● Draw an arc under each word root. ● Write the word for each definition.

1. _____ together as one; the _____ states

2. _____ a type of bicycle with only one wheel

3. _____ making the same sounds at the same time

4. _____ always the same; not changing

● Write the meanings for the word roots.

one	sound	wheel	

5. **cycl** _____   6. **uni** _____   7. **son** _____

- -

(TEST 35 VIS, VID)   visible   video   invisible   vision

● Draw an arc under each word root. ● Write the word for each definition.

1. _____ able to be seen

2. _____ not able to be seen

3. _____ picture part, or what is seen, on television

4. _____ the ability to see; eyesight

● Write the meanings for the word roots.

see	able to	not	

5. **vis** _____   6. **in** _____   7. **ible** _____

- -

PART 2
TEST
ANSWERS

Test, Answers

TEST 1: **act** **re act** **in act** ive **inter act**
1. act 2. inactive 3. react 4. interact 5. again 6. to do 7. between 8. in

TEST 2: **anim**al **anim**ate **magn**animous **in anim**ate
1. animate 2. animal 3. magnanimous 4. inanimate 5. without 6. life, spirit 7. great

TEST 3: **aqua** tic **aqua naut** **aqu** e **duct** **aqu arium**
1. aqueduct 2. aquatic 3. aquarium 4. aquanaut 5. water 6. to lead 7. explorer 8. a place for

TEST 4: **hydr** o **phobia** **de hydr** ate **hydr** o electric **hydr**ant
1. hydrant 2. hydrophobia 3. hydroelectric 4. dehydrate 5. water 6. fear 7. remove

TEST 5: **art ist** **arti**san **art** **art** i **fic** ial
1. art 2. artificial 3. artist 4. artisan 5. make 6. skill 7. one who

TEST 6: **aud ible** **in aud ible** **aud**ition **aud**ience
1. inaudible 2. audible 3. audition 4. audience 5. hear 6. able to 7. not

TEST 7: **bi cycl**e **bio logy** **bio graph** y **bi lingu** al
1. bilingual 2. bicycle 3. biology 4. biography 5. life 6. write 7. study 8. language 9. circle 10. two

TEST 8: ac**cept** **inter cept** **cap able** **cap**ture
1. intercept 2. accept 3. capture 4. capable 5. take, receive 6. between 7. able to

TEST 9: **per cent** **cent**ury **cent enn** ial **bi cent enn** ial
1. century 2. centennial 3. bicentennial 4. percent 5. part 6. two 7. hundred 8. years

TEST 10: **un cert**ain **cert**ain **cert** ificate **cert** i **fy**
1. certain 2. uncertain 3. certify 4. certificate 5. sure 6. not 7. make

TEST 11: **chron**ic **chron** o **meter** **syn chron** ize **chron ology**
1. synchronize 2. chronometer 3. chronology 4. chronic 5. science 6. time 7. measure 8. together, same

TEST 12: **circ**us **circ**le **circ** um **vent** **circ** um **nav** igate
1. circumvent 2. circle 3. circus 4. circumnavigate 5. around 6. to go 7. sail

TEST 13: **com**bine **con**nect **com** m **uni** ty **con greg** ate **Test**
1. community 2. congregate 3. combine 4. connect 5. flock 6. with, together 7. one

Answers, Continued

TEST 14: __bi cycl__e   __re cycl__e   __cycl__ one   __cycl__e

1. cycle   2. recycle   3. bicycle   4. cyclone   5. two   6. circle   7. again

TEST 15: __dec ad__ e   __dec__ a __pod__   __dec athlon__   __dec__ imal

1. decade   2. decimal   3. decapod   4. decathlon   5. ten   6. contest
7. foot   8. group

TEST 16: __demo crat__ ic   __demo cracy__   __pan dem__ ic   __epi dem__ ic

1. democratic   2. democracy   3. pandemic   4. epidemic   5. government   6. among
7. all   8. the people

TEST 17: __contra dict__   __dict__ at __or__   __dict__ ate   __pre dict__

1. dictator   2. predict   3. contradict   4. dictate   5. against   6. speak
7. one who   8. before

TEST 18: __equ__al   __un equal__   __equi lat__ eral   __equ__ality

1. equal   2. unequal   3. equality   4. equilateral   5. side   6. not   7. equal, same

TEST 19: __ex tend__   __ex claim__   __ex pel ex__it

1. exit   2. expel   3. exclaim   4. extend   5. out, from   6. stretch   7. drive, push   8. cry out

TEST 20: de __fin__e   __fini__sh   __con fin__e   __in fin__ ite

1. infinite   2. finish   3. confine   4. define   5. together   6. not   7. finish, end, limit

TEST 21: __flor__a   __flor ist__   __Flor__ida   __flor__ i __cult__ ure

1. Florida   2. florist   3. flora   4. floriculture   5. one who   6. cultivate   7. flower

TEST 22: __biblio graph__ y   __auto bio graph__ y   __bio graph__ y   __auto graph__

1. autograph   2. biography   3. autobiography   4. bibliography   5. life   6. write, draw
7. book   8. self

TEST 23: __hosp__ital   __host__age   __hosp__ ital __ity__   __host__el

1. hostel   2. hospitality   3. hostage   4. hospital   5. stranger, enemy   6. guest house

TEST 24: __zo ology__   __bio logy__   __eco logy__   __chron ology__

1. biology   2. zoology   3. ecology   4. chronology   5. time   6. environment
7. animal   8. study of, science of

TEST 25: **Medi** eval   **medi** an   **inter medi** ate   **medi terr** anean

1. Medieval 2. median 3. mediterranean 4. intermediate 5. between 6.. middle
7. land

TEST 26: **nov**ice   **re nov** ate   **nov**el   **in nov** ation

1. novice 2. novel 3. renovate 4. innovation 5. into 6. new 7. again

TEST 27: **homo nym**   **syn onym**   **ant onym**   an **onym**ous

1. anonymous 2. synonym 3. antonym 4. homonym 5. same 6. name, word
7. opposite 8 without

TEST 28: **omni potent**   **omni vor**e   **pan orama**   **pan** a **cea**

1. panorama 2. omnipotent 3. panacea 4. omnivore 5. all 6. to eat 7. view
8.. cure 9. powerful

TEST 29: **bi ped**   **ped**al   **ped** i **cure**   **ped** estrian

1. pedal 2. pedestrian 3. biped 4. pedicure 5. two 6. foot 7. care

TEST 30: **prim**itive **pri** or **ity**   **pri**mate   **prim ary**

1. primitive 2. primate 3. priority 4. primary 5. relating to 6. state of 7. first

TEST 31: **in tens** ity **ex tend**   **tens**e   **hyper tens** ion

1. tense 2. extend 3. hypertension 4. intensity 5. out 6. above, over
7. stretch, strain

TEST 32: **terr** itory   **terr arium**   terr ace   **medi terr** anean

1. terrace 2. territory 3. mediterranean 4. terrarium 5. land 6. middle
7. a place for

TEST 33: **ex tract**   **tract**or   **at tract**   **dis tract**

1. tractor 2. attract 3. extract 4. distract 5. out 6. to
7. away 8. draw, pull

TEST 34: **uni** son   **uni cycl** e   **un**i form **uni** ted

1. united 2. unicycle 3. unison 4. uniform 5. wheel 6.. one 7. sound

TEST 35: **vis ible** **vid**eo   **in vis ible**   **vis** ion

1. visible 2. invisible 3. video 4. vision 5. see 6. not 7. able to

PART 3

WORD SEARCH PUZZLES

WORD SEARCH 1, LESSONS 1, 2, 3

act	inactive	react	interact	animal
animate	inanimate	magnanimous	aquatic	aquarium
aqueduct	aquanaut			

EXTRA CREDIT: Make an arc under the word roots in the word box.

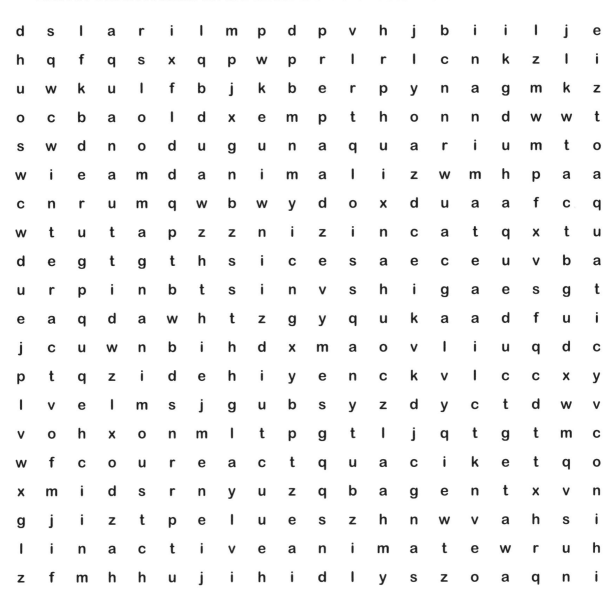

```
d  s  l  a  r  i  l  m  p  d  p  v  h  j  b  i  i  l  j  e
h  q  f  q  s  x  q  p  w  p  r  l  r  l  c  n  k  z  l  i
u  w  k  u  l  f  b  j  k  b  e  r  p  y  n  a  g  m  k  z
o  c  b  a  o  l  d  x  e  m  p  t  h  o  n  n  d  w  w  t
s  w  d  n  o  d  u  g  u  n  a  q  u  a  r  i  u  m  t  o
w  i  e  a  m  d  a  n  i  m  a  l  i  z  w  m  h  p  a  a
c  n  r  u  m  q  w  b  w  y  d  o  x  d  u  a  a  f  c  q
w  t  u  t  a  p  z  z  n  i  z  i  n  c  a  t  q  x  t  u
d  e  g  t  g  t  h  s  i  c  e  s  a  e  c  e  u  v  b  a
u  r  p  i  n  b  t  s  i  n  v  s  h  i  g  a  e  s  g  t
e  a  q  d  a  w  h  t  z  g  y  q  u  k  a  a  d  f  u  i
j  c  u  w  n  b  i  h  d  x  m  a  o  v  l  i  u  q  d  c
p  t  q  z  i  d  e  h  i  y  e  n  c  k  v  l  c  c  x  y
l  v  e  l  m  s  j  g  u  b  s  y  z  d  y  c  t  d  w  v
v  o  h  x  o  n  m  l  t  p  g  t  l  j  q  t  g  t  m  c
w  f  c  o  u  r  e  a  c  t  q  u  a  c  i  k  e  t  q  o
x  m  i  d  s  r  n  y  u  z  q  b  a  g  e  n  t  x  v  n
g  j  i  z  t  p  e  l  u  e  s  z  h  n  w  v  a  h  s  i
l  i  n  a  c  t  i  v  e  a  n  i  m  a  t  e  w  r  u  h
z  f  m  h  h  u  j  i  h  i  d  l  y  s  z  o  a  q  n  i
```

Write the words you found on the lines.

_____

_____

_____

_____

```
          q                               n
          u                               a
          a                               n
          n               a q u a r i u m
   i      a       a n i m a l       m     a a
   n      u m                       a a   c q
   t      t a                       t q   t u
   e      g                         e u   a
   r      n                         e     t
   a      a                         d     i
   c      n                         u     c
   t      i                         c
          m                         t
          o
          u r e a c t
          s

   i n a c t i v e a n i m a t e
```

WORD SEARCH 2, LESSONS 4, 5, 6

hydrate	dehydrate	hydrophobia	hydroelectric	art
artist	artisan	artificial	audible	inaudible
audience	audition			

EXTRA CREDIT. Make an arc under the word roots in the word box.

```
h a m c c n v w l n g n q q z q i s p i
y u l w p u j n a v z r v a k l v i m u
d d p h s l c p n c f s e u l z v g k k
r i d x x o x x g t i r m d a g g j c k
o b k g z t b o o x a b y i r d x y c r
p l f k e z k z q a m p d e t e h k u u
h e i j e e t p f z m x f n i h o d r j
o z h q g w x p m l h h b c s y a n l l
b u y n s j k h z a y h x e t d n j h k
i q l i w b f m l c d b x n l r p q p m
a p n q x w w q s i r f l j z a r e k w
a i e o f c e v t n a g w u y t e j l o
g c p j r k h e z v n x l o w e s v b h
n h y d r o e l e c t r i c a z x r y u
a r t i f i c i a l c m a e r y r t x c
q c p x w j j m x z x a h i t w z m g f
k t x i n a u d i b l e w t i w f q h f
s q u l a u d i t i o n t q s k u w o s
t e b d b x p c w o i v f d a c x d r p
i a f e k w s l u e r v p c n p x a v h
```

Write the words you found on the lines.

_____

_____

_____

_____

WORD SEARCH 2, ANSWER KEY, LESSONS 1, 2, 3

```
h   a
y   u
d   i                         a
r                             u
o   b                         d   a
p   l                         i   r   d
h   e                         e   t   e
o               h             n   i   h
b               y             c   s   y
i               d             e   t   d
a               r                     r
                a                     a
                n                     t
                                      e
    h  y  d  r  o  e  l  e  c  t  r  i  c  a
    r  t  i  f  i  c  i  a  l             r
                                          t
       i  n  a  u  d  i  b  l  e  w       i
       a  u  d  i  t  i  o  n             s
                                          a
                                          n
```

WORD SEARCH 3, LESSONS 7, 8, 9

bicycle   bilingual   biology   biography   accept

intercept   capable   capture   cent   centennial

bicentennial   percent

EXTRA CREDIT. Make an arc under the word roots in the word box.

```
p  a  o  h  j  f  e  c  e  n  t  e  n  n  i  a  l  l  d  z
e  s  y  w  d  k  f  c  a  p  a  b  l  e  g  i  s  h  k  k
r  m  r  d  b  i  o  g  r  a  p  h  y  h  x  f  x  i  a  k
c  u  z  a  c  c  e  p  t  u  d  z  b  k  i  u  p  o  j  s
e  v  p  b  e  w  f  g  h  y  a  k  l  i  y  j  l  e  q  g
n  u  s  q  w  q  b  s  r  y  o  f  d  u  l  d  x  u  b  i
t  k  a  c  g  z  g  o  k  d  r  k  r  y  a  e  u  o  d  b
a  k  r  q  k  z  a  u  h  c  p  h  r  r  b  n  c  e  n  t
w  s  v  q  g  r  d  t  e  t  o  a  s  u  e  y  e  z  d  o
u  u  w  z  n  u  f  z  e  e  e  o  j  j  g  d  a  d  t  l
h  y  w  p  l  e  z  e  o  u  y  h  x  o  s  w  r  o  s  e
u  c  v  a  d  e  r  o  j  b  i  o  l  o  g  y  c  w  h  y
t  s  e  i  z  h  a  w  k  d  n  p  j  j  t  x  x  x  f  o
k  i  o  j  d  u  x  n  t  g  t  t  w  f  t  q  o  f  g  n
b  i  l  i  n  g  u  a  l  k  e  b  i  i  c  i  t  x  d  d
k  a  n  h  y  a  w  g  n  w  r  g  s  i  b  l  w  l  k  x
s  a  f  q  s  v  z  d  b  i  c  e  n  t  e  n  n  i  a  l
e  f  d  j  b  i  c  y  c  l  e  c  a  p  t  u  r  e  m  u
m  r  i  a  x  j  i  v  x  k  p  v  i  v  p  u  f  s  r  b
t  v  y  m  b  z  h  h  c  u  t  w  i  l  t  l  x  x  g  x
```

Write the words you found on the lines.

_____

_____

_____

_____

WORD SEARCH 3, ANSWER KEY, LESSONS 7, 8, 9

```
p                    c e n t e n n i a l
e                    c a p a b l e
r          b i o g r a p h y
c       a c c e p t
e
n
t                                        c e n t


                  b i o l o g y
                  n
                  t
b i l i n g u a l k e
                  r
                  b i c e n t e n n i a l
          b i c y c l e c a p t u r e
                  p
                  t
```

©2014, GLAVACH & ASSOCIATES

WORD SEARCH 4, LESSONS 10, 11, 12

certain   uncertain   certify certificate   chronic

chronology   synchronize chronometer circle circus

circumvent   circumnavigate

EXTRA CREDIT. Make an arc under the word roots in the word box.

```
b  c  r  x  c  m  t  d  r  d  i  v  q  t  j  n  a  d  o  q
a  x  w  b  e  t  a  c  i  f  i  t  r  e  c  v  p  i  y  z
y  u  r  j  x  b  t  c  m  s  t  j  c  q  k  t  l  k  c  j
r  j  x  h  i  y  k  i  d  u  d  z  g  k  y  x  e  c  i  f
e  k  r  d  s  g  f  r  k  c  v  o  o  s  k  w  x  r  r  w
m  j  n  t  y  r  m  c  t  r  e  a  o  c  n  c  f  e  c  k
y  h  r  y  n  t  j  u  o  i  y  s  t  v  e  n  a  t  u  c
g  z  e  f  c  p  n  m  l  c  c  e  r  t  a  i  n  e  m  c
o  n  k  m  h  f  i  n  z  r  c  h  u  y  g  r  g  m  v  h
l  l  f  i  r  d  a  a  y  r  c  l  k  y  q  p  z  o  e  r
o  d  r  q  o  i  t  v  t  l  x  v  q  s  p  p  w  n  n  o
n  n  b  j  n  w  r  i  g  t  b  t  q  h  t  c  w  o  t  n
o  u  s  m  i  p  e  g  q  m  c  d  v  s  l  g  e  r  d  i
r  l  f  d  z  j  c  a  k  b  m  q  j  b  j  e  y  h  s  c
h  n  v  y  e  e  n  t  p  a  b  n  y  x  y  l  f  c  q  e
c  c  d  o  x  o  u  e  b  d  b  q  p  d  f  c  i  w  s  c
p  b  q  r  y  w  e  g  k  n  l  b  o  a  q  r  t  w  n  p
v  f  r  i  r  t  f  b  k  o  p  g  n  o  l  i  r  m  o  u
o  w  a  b  j  t  u  h  y  p  u  g  d  l  g  c  e  m  c  y
k  v  k  j  k  n  x  c  p  d  n  d  v  u  f  v  c  e  s  v
```

Write the words you found on the lines.

_____

_____

_____

_____

WORD SEARCH 4, ANSWER KEY, LESSONS 10, 11, 12

```
            e t a c i f i t r e c                        c
                c       s                                i
                i       u                r               r
        s       r       c                e               c
        y       c       r                t               u
y       n       u       i                m               m       c
g       c   n m c   c e r t a i n         o       e y h   c
o       h   i n                          n       t   r   h
l       r   a a                          o       o   n   r
o       n   t v                          r   e y h c     o
n       i   r i                          h   l f i c     n
o       z   e g                              c t r       i
r       e   n a                              r i e       c
h           u t                              i t c
c             e                              c r
                                               e
                                               c
```

WORD SEARCH 5, LESSONS 13, 14, 15

connect	congregate	combine	community	cycle
recycle	bicycle	cyclone	decade	decathlon
decimal	decapod			

EXTRA CREDIT. Make an arc under the word roots in the word box.

```
p  o  x  x  d  x  a  e  m  i  z  y  f  p  s  z  z  g  o  p
h  c  r  p  n  o  p  k  r  e  l  h  t  u  t  d  v  x  d  u
k  o  d  e  c  a  t  h  l  o  n  o  d  t  v  d  o  q  y  u
k  n  w  z  s  x  e  c  c  j  k  y  z  a  p  k  u  y  h  a
t  n  l  k  x  q  t  l  o  n  p  f  c  c  m  h  h  y  b  w
g  e  d  k  c  q  a  w  u  s  c  j  o  i  x  e  h  t  o  d
e  c  e  e  g  e  g  o  l  v  s  n  c  p  e  o  e  i  y  w
u  t  c  s  t  a  e  e  c  l  a  t  g  r  l  g  n  n  v  z
g  e  a  o  b  u  r  g  y  r  s  k  o  h  c  w  o  u  a  n
i  t  d  g  x  j  g  q  c  f  k  v  q  b  y  i  l  m  z  y
p  c  e  s  n  o  n  o  l  t  n  o  a  v  c  o  c  m  u  w
b  s  z  e  k  z  o  b  e  k  b  x  j  f  i  y  y  o  h  l
o  i  d  n  g  z  c  e  l  c  y  c  e  r  b  y  c  c  u  y
k  d  s  i  m  h  o  h  k  o  d  g  n  p  u  c  z  v  s  i
d  x  w  f  l  x  g  b  e  o  i  q  e  n  i  b  m  o  c  t
c  w  n  y  k  d  e  c  i  m  a  l  i  w  v  o  r  y  y  d
v  z  j  d  e  c  a  p  o  d  b  v  e  y  w  p  z  y  m  r
```

Write the words you found on the lines.

_____

_____

_____

_____

WORD SEARCH 5, ANSWER KEY, LESSONS 13, 14, 15

```
c
o d e c a t h l o n
n             e
n             t                           y
e d           a                           t
c e           g                 e     e   i
t c           e     c           l     n   n
  a           r     y           c     o   u
  d           g     c           y     l   m
  e           n     l           c     c   m
              o     e           i     y   o
              c e l c y c e r b       c   c
                                e n i b m o c
        d e c i m a l
      d e c a p o d
```

WORD SEARCH 6, LESSONS 16, 17, 18

democracy	democratic	epidemic	pandemic	dictate
dictator	predict	contradict	equal unequal	
equality	equilateral			

EXTRA CREDIT. Make an arc under the word roots in the word box.

```
s  n  s  m  a  j  i  d  c  r  p  b  q  p  p  r  e  z  u  b
s  n  d  h  n  b  s  t  n  y  v  j  k  j  a  o  f  p  y  u
p  s  t  k  t  k  h  q  y  e  q  u  i  l  a  t  e  r  a  l
f  u  d  c  n  v  n  i  w  i  t  x  g  x  m  a  x  k  w  d
h  l  f  o  n  k  u  q  o  q  z  l  m  e  x  t  y  z  c  w
i  c  k  n  r  o  g  f  r  l  m  v  f  p  a  c  u  c  w  z
c  u  v  t  i  r  z  b  w  u  i  c  g  i  f  i  n  f  c  y
s  v  d  r  f  f  s  i  f  a  j  z  o  d  y  d  e  x  l  y
a  u  h  a  b  t  y  m  s  x  g  k  e  e  h  f  q  p  a  u
i  d  h  d  u  v  y  p  o  j  j  j  h  m  c  r  u  y  u  l
r  b  d  i  z  d  f  n  v  k  f  q  y  i  i  v  a  q  q  d
m  w  j  c  d  e  m  o  c  r  a  t  i  c  m  h  l  e  e  c
e  g  y  t  u  d  e  m  o  c  r  a  c  y  e  j  v  c  e  f
f  z  v  f  j  j  p  j  b  y  v  m  f  x  d  m  k  r  k  n
t  b  g  s  a  h  a  t  c  i  d  e  r  p  n  q  d  c  q  z
r  a  r  y  d  x  q  v  s  b  x  o  f  f  a  c  m  w  g  o
q  m  x  y  t  i  l  a  y  q  e  f  j  t  p  j  x  t  s  v
c  c  u  k  u  q  b  l  f  n  w  u  s  y  v  i  m  r  j  q
j  e  m  q  b  q  b  q  r  u  u  d  i  c  t  a  t  e  s  u
j  d  k  d  v  k  f  j  i  w  v  r  p  u  x  x  m  o  k  v
```

Write the words you found on the lines.

_____

_____

_____

_____

WORD SEARCH 6, ANSWER KEY, LESSONS 16, 17, 18

```
                                        r
                                        o
                    e  q  u  i  l  a  t  e  r  a  l
      c                           a
      o                     e     t
      n                     p     c  u
      t                     i     i  n
      r                     d     d  e     l
      a                     e        q     a
      d                     m  c     u     u
      i                     i  i     a     q
      c  d  e  m  o  c  r  a  t  i  c  m     l     e
      t     d  e  m  o  c  r  a  c  y  e
                                     d
            t  c  i  d  e  r  p  n  a
                                  a
      y  t  i  l  a  u  q  e      p

                     d  i  c  t  a  t  e
```

WORD SEARCH 7, LESSONS 19, 20, 21

exit	expel	extend exclaim		finish
infinite		define confine		flora florist
Florida		floriculture		

EXTRA CREDIT. Make an arc under the word roots in the word box.

```
e  p  l  w  i  t  w  e  t  x  t  h  h  t  d  w  p  w  s  k
d  y  t  x  g  p  g  e  e  d  i  h  p  p  h  q  x  a  f  a
d  p  e  y  a  o  j  x  g  z  g  z  m  o  w  e  y  e  m  k
p  h  s  i  n  i  f  c  z  l  d  d  u  x  c  k  i  j  d  f
w  n  t  v  y  x  q  l  q  k  e  k  b  w  s  q  k  s  z  z
o  i  t  x  v  r  d  a  e  t  i  n  i  f  n  i  d  b  f  v
g  z  q  e  x  w  y  i  t  a  d  m  k  s  h  j  e  u  q  y
k  z  p  k  s  f  r  m  a  w  z  j  m  m  c  i  f  v  x  m
a  g  x  b  r  f  l  o  r  i  d  a  v  d  d  f  i  w  d  p
i  r  f  u  l  o  p  n  x  k  g  e  h  v  d  o  n  e  m  e
j  r  e  x  t  e  n  d  g  u  v  m  l  e  f  k  e  f  j  v
d  u  o  c  z  f  d  f  s  a  i  h  h  n  t  q  v  l  n  q
l  v  s  o  h  a  b  k  g  n  p  z  u  i  v  e  h  o  x  s
e  b  e  r  a  r  o  v  d  e  r  p  i  f  y  j  v  r  s  x
p  l  w  r  o  o  a  c  d  y  z  d  r  n  z  v  p  i  m  q
x  f  m  h  j  l  k  e  y  m  e  j  x  o  s  k  q  s  y  u
e  y  l  q  p  f  n  n  a  a  m  g  g  c  e  v  t  t  m  x
h  x  n  p  n  p  g  d  j  n  e  u  j  c  h  m  c  o  z  l
f  l  o  r  i  c  u  l  t  u  r  e  h  t  q  a  u  u  h  c
v  x  k  j  y  d  e  j  a  e  k  p  p  b  j  i  t  i  x  e
```

Write the words you found on the lines.

_____

_____

_____

_____

WORD SEARCH 7, ANSWER KEY, LESSONS 19, 20, 21

```
                        e
                        e
                        x
        h  s  i  n  i  f  c
                        l
                        a  e  t  i  n  i  f  n  i  d
                        i                          e
                        m                          f
           f  l  o  r  i  d  a                     i
                                                   n
     e  x  t  e  n  d                 e            e  f
                                      n               l
  l                    a              i               o
  e                    r              f               r
  p                    o              n               i
  x                    l              o               s
  e                    f              c               t

        l  o  r  i  c  u  l  t  u  r  e

                                      t  i  x  e
```

WORD SEARCH 8, LESSONS 22, 23, 24

biography   autobiography   autograph   bibliography   hospital

hospitality   hostage   hostelbiology   chronology

ecology   zoology

EXTRA CREDIT. Make an arc under the word roots in the word box.

```
q  i  j  a  z  y  l  m  z  o  o  l  o  g  y  u  b  a  r  o
m  l  r  u  o  j  h  j  i  k  s  c  l  a  x  l  a  u  c  v
e  w  o  t  e  u  o  x  p  h  w  f  g  p  d  f  h  t  x  a
r  p  d  o  m  n  s  x  g  r  k  l  k  d  p  e  a  o  x  k
z  u  n  g  g  h  t  e  d  h  u  p  m  t  t  z  e  b  j  d
t  r  h  r  r  o  e  g  z  v  m  p  f  u  h  l  f  i  t  z
b  r  r  a  u  j  l  a  j  y  d  i  p  h  y  g  j  o  p  k
c  t  j  p  y  o  i  t  n  p  y  q  n  v  t  a  p  g  l  k
h  x  k  h  k  x  h  s  m  j  x  w  s  b  i  o  y  r  p  y
t  c  k  l  g  u  o  o  v  r  c  v  j  i  l  q  n  a  i  g
z  n  k  v  t  h  v  h  y  r  n  v  r  o  a  o  a  p  x  o
q  z  w  p  w  e  c  o  l  o  g  y  h  g  t  v  g  h  y  l
o  c  v  e  a  j  o  l  x  u  z  w  e  r  i  m  y  y  g  o
z  i  d  n  d  e  g  y  d  e  i  k  b  a  p  y  q  z  f  i
z  m  x  k  y  r  c  n  p  v  l  n  u  p  s  r  r  o  d  b
y  w  e  z  p  i  f  a  w  b  a  b  n  h  o  r  l  k  p  i
c  z  x  y  g  o  l  o  n  o  r  h  c  y  h  d  t  j  l  h
l  i  c  a  a  b  y  h  p  a  r  g  o  i  l  b  i  b  f  m
i  q  k  s  r  k  l  k  z  h  o  s  p  i  t  a  l  n  x  f
r  l  t  y  y  q  p  x  l  t  j  u  u  s  d  d  r  h  z  t
```

Write the words you found on the lines.

_____

_____

_____

_____

©2014, GLAVACH & ASSOCIATES

WORD SEARCH 8, ANSWER KEY, LESSONS 22, 23, 24

```
a                 z   o   l   o   g   y               a
u           h                                         u
t           o                                         t
o           s       e                                 b
g           t       g                                 i
r           e       a               y                 o
a           l       t               t                 g
p               x   s           b   i                 r           y
h   k               o           i   l                 a           g
                    h           o   a                 p           o
        e   c   o   l   o   g   y   h   g   t           h           l
                                g   r   i               y           o
                                r   p                               i
                                a   s                               b
                                p   o
                                h   h
y   g   o   l   o   n   o   r   h   c   y   h
    b   y   h   p   a   r   g   o   i   l   b   i   b
            h   o   s   p   i   t   a   l
```

©2014, GLAVACH & ASSOCIATES

WORD SEARCH 9, LESSONS 25, 26, 27

median	intermediate	Medieval	Mediterranean	novel
novice	innovation	renovation	synonym	antonym
homonym	anonymous			

EXTRA CREDIT. Make an arc under the word roots in the word box.

```
n  g  b  a  f  a  m  q  m  a  c  h  u  v  u  e  d  b  g  g
o  f  c  s  e  k  w  k  f  q  q  a  u  t  i  d  n  v  j  b
v  u  g  t  h  g  k  t  f  e  o  v  q  s  r  s  u  u  i  g
e  a  p  v  h  d  x  a  c  c  z  a  j  r  r  s  i  w  t  r
l  j  w  a  e  x  k  r  e  n  o  v  a  t  i  o  n  w  q  b
u  d  g  h  f  y  a  n  o  n  y  m  o  u  s  l  k  h  x  u
r  s  q  q  i  m  v  j  x  g  c  s  x  z  s  a  l  t  m  w
g  n  a  n  t  o  n  y  m  h  o  m  o  n  y  m  t  y  k  l
e  t  a  i  d  e  m  r  e  t  n  i  x  q  a  n  z  t  x  g
a  n  m  c  g  e  k  v  i  p  m  c  g  r  m  m  n  d  s  q
w  h  s  z  d  f  x  j  u  g  e  h  t  q  u  m  y  t  g  m
o  p  y  i  n  n  o  v  a  t  i  o  n  n  r  i  r  k  s  n
w  p  n  z  h  l  r  j  r  j  t  m  r  a  b  w  g  q  u  b
h  e  o  m  y  b  o  f  c  l  n  m  z  i  v  p  d  l  y  o
w  s  n  k  i  k  z  j  l  q  e  p  j  d  s  y  e  o  s  g
q  j  y  q  z  p  s  a  c  v  o  e  v  e  p  o  v  q  p  b
u  m  m  j  a  u  k  e  n  p  o  z  f  m  f  i  j  s  f  p
c  e  i  m  e  d  i  t  e  r  r  a  n  e  a  n  z  f  m  e
l  k  s  q  n  o  v  i  c  e  g  o  l  g  a  s  a  p  i  d
z  x  o  t  q  h  q  l  a  v  e  i  d  e  m  r  d  u  z  y
```

Write the words you found on the lines.

_____

_____

_____

_____

```
n
o
v
e
l                         r  e  n  o  v  a  t  i  o  n
                          a  n  o  n  y  m  o  u  s
              a  n  t  o  n  y  m  h  o  m  o  n  y  m
    e  t  a  i  d  e  m  r  e  t  n  i
          m
          s
          y  i  n  n  o  v  a  t  i  o  n     n
          n                                  a
          o                                  i
          n                                  d
          y                                  e
          m                                  m
              m  e  d  i  t  e  r  r  a  n  e  a  n
              n  o  v  i  c  e
                    l  a  v  e  i  d  e  m
```

WORD SEARCH 10, LESSONS 28, 29, 30

omnipotent   omnivore   panacea   panorama   pedal

pedestrian   biped pedicure   primary   primitive

primate   priority

EXTRA CREDIT. Make an arc under the word roots in the word box.

```
o  p  e  d  i  c  u  r  e  e  l  a  d  e  p  a  c  l  x  q
k  x  o  r  p  b  k  q  g  q  v  s  h  b  p  k  y  p  p  w
y  j  f  v  v  w  a  o  m  k  o  k  o  y  d  l  t  h  r  z
k  t  b  q  q  i  n  m  f  x  b  r  g  r  p  d  n  f  i  a
b  x  j  d  y  e  p  h  v  v  p  n  d  d  b  e  e  m  m  d
b  c  f  s  g  g  r  x  z  k  u  a  e  h  g  p  t  k  i  j
q  k  b  i  l  v  i  a  e  g  f  z  t  p  r  i  o  n  t  h
a  r  c  t  z  a  m  t  c  w  n  t  a  r  m  b  p  m  i  y
l  d  q  g  c  i  a  h  r  u  a  l  m  i  x  s  i  a  v  d
h  l  h  y  a  x  r  e  c  s  i  d  i  o  n  t  n  e  e  m
e  r  n  v  m  p  y  s  y  o  r  u  r  r  q  j  m  i  p  q
c  s  f  d  a  f  u  b  r  p  t  o  p  i  c  z  o  e  o  t
x  t  c  e  r  z  l  j  q  a  s  z  w  t  c  x  l  e  m  x
q  y  a  j  o  c  t  f  b  b  e  e  y  y  q  u  r  c  n  j
l  l  e  b  n  m  i  z  f  s  d  n  h  n  y  u  o  n  i  p
j  v  c  z  a  l  e  y  m  q  e  t  w  r  a  c  c  p  v  s
h  v  a  d  p  w  c  d  o  b  p  h  j  f  s  e  a  c  o  i
f  m  n  e  t  o  g  d  e  c  m  x  m  p  z  n  g  i  r  m
j  g  a  l  b  p  a  i  c  z  n  c  e  q  x  m  w  o  e  m
t  s  p  h  k  z  j  b  x  m  c  g  g  q  e  a  z  b  c  j
```

Write the words you found on the lines.

_____

_____

_____

_____

WORD SEARCH 10, ANSWER KEY, LESSONS 28, 29, 30

```
p e d i c u r e   l a   d   e p
                                                p
                                    t           r
                            d   n           i
                            e   e           m
            p               e   e               p   t           i
            r       e       p   t           i
            i       t   p   i   o           t
            m   n   a   r   b   p           i
            a   a   m   i       i           v
    a   r   i   i   o           n           e
    m   y   r   r   r           m
    a   t   p   i           o           o
    r   s   t                           m
a   o   e   y                           n
e   n   d                               i
c   a   e                               v
a   p   p                               o
n                                       r
a                                       e
            p
```

©2014, GLAVACH & ASSOCIATES

WORD SEARCH 11, LESSONS 31, 32, 34

extend   tense intensity   hypertension   terrace

territory   Mediterranean   terrarium   tractor   attract

distract   extract

EXTRA CREDIT. Make an arc under the word roots in the word box.

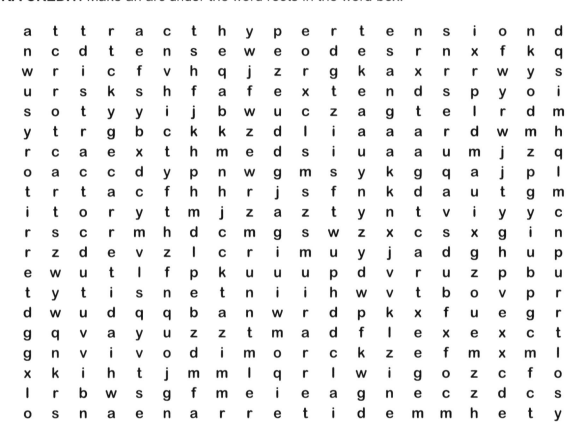

```
a  t  t  r  a  c  t  h  y  p  e  r  t  e  n  s  i  o  n  d
n  c  d  t  e  n  s  e  w  e  o  d  e  s  r  n  x  f  k  q
w  r  i  c  f  v  h  q  j  z  r  g  k  a  x  r  r  w  y  s
u  r  s  k  s  h  f  a  f  e  x  t  e  n  d  s  p  y  o  i
s  o  t  y  y  i  j  b  w  u  c  z  a  g  t  e  l  r  d  m
y  t  r  g  b  c  k  k  z  d  l  i  a  a  r  d  w  m  h
r  c  a  e  x  t  h  m  e  d  s  i  u  a  a  u  m  j  z  q
o  a  c  c  d  y  p  n  w  g  m  s  y  k  g  q  a  j  p  l
t  r  t  a  c  f  h  h  r  j  s  f  n  k  d  a  u  t  g  m
i  t  o  r  y  t  m  j  z  a  z  t  y  n  t  v  i  y  y  c
r  s  c  r  m  h  d  c  m  g  s  w  z  x  c  s  x  g  i  n
r  z  d  e  v  z  l  c  r  i  m  u  y  j  a  d  g  h  u  p
e  w  u  t  l  f  p  k  u  u  u  p  d  v  r  u  z  p  b  u
t  y  t  i  s  n  e  t  n  i  i  h  w  v  t  b  o  v  p  r
d  w  u  d  q  q  b  a  n  w  r  d  p  k  x  f  u  e  g  r
g  q  v  a  y  u  z  z  t  m  a  d  f  l  e  x  e  x  c  t
g  n  v  i  v  o  d  i  m  o  r  c  k  z  e  f  m  x  m  l
x  k  i  h  t  j  m  m  l  q  r  l  w  i  g  o  z  c  f  o
l  r  b  w  s  g  f  m  e  i  e  a  g  n  e  c  z  d  c  s
o  s  n  a  e  n  a  r  r  e  t  i  d  e  m  m  h  e  t  y
```

Write the words you found on the lines.

_____

_____

_____

_____

WORD SEARCH 11, ANSWER KEY, LESSONS 1, 2, 3

```
a t t r a c t h y p e r t e n s i o n d
    d   t e n s e
    r   i
    r   s                   e x t e n d
    o   t
y   t   r
r   c   a   e
o   a   c   c
t   r   t   a
i   t   r                                   t
r       r                                   c
r       e                       m           a
e       t                       u           r
t y t i s n e t n i              i           t
                                 r           x
                                 a           e
                                 r
                                 r
                                 e
    n a e n a r r e t i d e m
```

WORD SEARCH 12, LESSONS 33, 34, 35

tractor	attract	distract	extract	united
uniform	unicycle	unison	vision	visible
invisible	video			

EXTRA CREDIT. Make an arc under the word roots in the word box.

```
j  p  w  g  a  y  b  e  i  t  v  h  k  t  v  k  u  j  t  h
m  b  d  e  m  y  u  l  k  m  z  f  p  w  i  b  k  k  t  c
l  l  n  d  y  o  i  c  e  g  h  j  l  d  w  x  d  s  o  e
t  e  e  i  h  r  l  y  d  n  s  u  g  w  x  e  u  o  i  v
l  z  x  m  o  z  j  c  m  z  n  f  x  t  i  t  n  e  f  d
y  g  t  o  d  i  p  i  e  r  q  q  a  c  z  z  i  v  k  w
g  d  r  q  j  y  d  n  l  u  b  s  q  a  f  n  s  s  m  k
n  c  a  q  z  b  s  u  a  t  o  i  c  r  v  b  o  k  r  e
o  a  c  j  d  h  h  j  f  s  z  a  e  t  i  q  n  f  o  e
i  h  t  w  a  r  i  h  p  e  t  q  t  t  d  e  m  k  t  l
s  k  q  w  u  e  r  a  x  l  y  x  u  a  e  a  t  i  c  b
i  t  s  f  w  h  t  w  w  b  j  d  n  s  o  h  o  u  a  i
v  k  l  u  s  u  g  g  h  i  d  o  i  r  a  z  a  p  r  s
m  p  v  o  g  n  p  f  o  s  e  m  f  m  f  m  g  u  t  i
l  t  x  f  u  l  e  e  m  i  t  r  o  c  e  f  o  f  d  v
f  b  y  k  i  h  w  g  f  v  i  y  r  v  a  x  d  z  c  n
k  o  t  g  m  q  c  u  u  j  n  o  m  f  h  e  x  h  c  i
j  r  d  i  s  t  r  a  c  t  u  d  u  b  x  k  y  t  y  x
k  y  i  o  t  f  y  f  o  w  i  d  g  b  m  o  x  p  h
x  x  l  s  r  s  p  x  k  c  g  g  n  y  m  k  t  g  l  m
```

Write the words you found on the lines.

_____

_____

_____

_____

WORD SEARCH 12, ANSWER KEY, LESSONS 33, 34, 35

```
                           e
                           l
                           c
        e                  y                          u
        x                  c              t           n
        t                  i              c           i
        r                  n              a           s
n       a                  u              r    v    o    k    r
o       c                               t    i    n    f    o    e
i       t                        e       t    d    m    k    t    l
s                                l       u    a    e              c    b
i                                b       n         o              a    i
v                                i    d  i                         r    s
                                 s    e  f                         t    i
                                 i    t  o                              v
                                 v    i  r                              n
                                 n       m                              i
        d    i    s    t    r    a    c    t    u
```

PART 4

WORD ROOT CONCENTRATION GAMES

Word Root Concentration Game 1, Lessons 1-8

Cut out the word cards. Place face down and match the pairs.
Say the sample words. (Extra credit for knowing underlined word root meanings.)

act active **in**active **re**act **inter**act	**anim** animal animate **in**animate **magn**animous	**aqu, aqua** aquatic aqu**arium** aque**duct** aqua**naut**	**hydr** hydrant **de**hydrate hydro**phobia** hydro**electric**
to do	**life, spirit**	**water**	**water**
art art art**ist** artisan arti**fici**al	**aud** aud**ible** inaud**ible** audience audition	**bi** bi**cyc**le bi**lingu**al **bio** bio**logy** bio**graph**y	**cap, cept** accept **inter**cept cap**able** capture
skill	**hear, listen**	**two life**	**take, receive**

Word Root Concentration Game 2, Lessons 9-16

Cut out the word cards. Place face down and match the pairs.
Say the sample words. (Extra credit for knowing underlined word root meanings.)

cent century cent**enn**ial **bi**cent**enn**ial **per**cent	**cert** certain **un**certain certi**fy** certificate	**chron** chronic chron**ology** **syn**chronize chrono**meter**	**circ, circum** circle circus circum**vent** circum**nav**igate
hundred	**certain, sure**	**time**	**around**
con, com connect con**greg**ate combine comm**unit**y	**cycl/e** cycle **re**cycle **bi**cycle cyclone	**dem/o** demo**cracy** demo**cratic** **epi**demic **pan**demic	**dec** dec**ade** dec**athlon** decimal deca**pod**
with, together	**circle, wheel**	**the people**	**ten**

Word Root Concentration Game 3, Lessons 17-24

Cut out the word cards. Place face down and match the pairs.
Say the sample words. (Extra credit for knowing underlined word root meanings.)

dict dictate dictat**or** **pre**dict **contra**dict	**equ** equal **un**equal equality equi**lat**eral	**ex** exit ex**pel** ex**tend** ex**claim**	**fin** finish **in**finite **de**fine **con**fine
speak, say	**equal, same**	**out, from**	**finish, end, limit**
flor flora flor**ist** Florida flori**cult**ure	**graph** **bio**graphy **autobio**graphy **auto**graph **biblio**graphy	**hosp** hospital hospitality **host** hostage hostel	**logy, ology** **bio**logy **chron**ology **eco**logy **zo**ology
flower	**write, draw**	**guest house** **stranger, enemy**	**study of, science of**

Word Root Concentration Game 4, Lessons 25 - 32

Cut out the word cards. Place face down and match the pairs.
Say the sample words. (Extra credit for knowing underlined word root meanings.)

medi median, medial **inter**mediate Medieval medi**terr**anean	**nov** novel novice **in**novation **re**novate	**nym, onym** **syn**onym **ant**onym **homo**nym **an**onymous	**omni** omni**poten**t omni**vor**e **pan** pana**cea** pan**orama**
middle	**new**	**name, word**	**all**
ped pedal pedestrian **bi**ped pedi**cure**	**pri, prim** prim**ary** primitive primate prior**ity**	**tend, tens** **ex**tend tense **in**tensity **hyper**tension	**terr** terrace territory **medi**terranean terr**arium**
foot, feet	**first**	**stretch, strain**	**land**

Word Root Concentration Game 4, (continued)
Cut out the word cards. Place face down and match the pairs.
Say the sample words. (Extra credit for knowing underlined word root meanings.)

tract tractor **at**tract **dis**tract **ex**tract	**uni** united uniform uni**cycl**e uni**son**	**vis, vid** vision vis**ible** **in**vis**ible** video	
draw, pull	**one**	**see**	

PART 5

READING AND MEANING

READING AND MEANING 1
(LESSONS 1-8, Student Reading Practice)

1. **act** (to do)   act   **in**active   **re**act   **inter**act

2. **anim** (life, spirit)   animal animate   **in**animate   **magn**animous

3. **aqu/a** (water)   aquaticaqu**arium**   aque**duct**   aqua**naut**

4. **hydr** (water)   hydrant   hydro**electric de**hydrate   hydro**phobia**

5. **art** (skill)   art   art**ist**   artisan   arti**fic**ial

6. **aud** (hear, listen)   aud**ible**   **in**aud**ible**   audience   audition

7. **bi** (two)   bi**cycl**ebi**lingu**al **bio** (life) bio**logy**   bio**graph**y

8. **cap, cept** (take, receive) capture cap**able**   accept   **inter**cept

READING AND MEANING 2

→

9. **cent** (hundred)   centurycent**enn**ial   **bi**cent**enn**ial   **per**cent

10. **cert** (certain, sure)   certain **un**certain   cert**ify**   certificate

11. **chron** (time)   chronicchron**ology**   **syn**chronize   chrono**meter**

12. **circ, circum** (around)   circle   circus   circum**vent**   circum**nav**igate

13. **con, com** (with, together) connect   con**greg**ate   combine   comm**uni**ty

14. **cycl** (circle, wheel)   cycle   **re**cycle   **bi**cycle   cyclone

15. **dec** (ten)   dec**a**de   dec**athlon**   decimal   deca**pod**

16. **dem/o** (the people) demo**cracy**   demo**crat**ic   **epi**demic   **pan**demic

→

READING AND MEANING 3
(LESSONS 17-25, Student Reading Practice)

17. **dict** (speak, say) dictate dictat**or** **pre**dict **contra**dict

18. **equ** (equal, same)**un**equal equal equality equi**lat**eral

19. **ex** (exit) exit ex**pel** ex**tend** ex**claim**

20. **fin** (finish, end, limit) finish **in**finite define **con**fine

21. **flor** (flower) flora flor**ist** Florida flori**cult**ure

22. **graph** (write, draw) **bio**graphy **auto**biography**auto**graph **biblio**graphy

23. **hosp** (guest house) hospital hospitality / **host (stranger, enemy)** hostage hostel

24. **logy, ology** (study of, science of) **bio**graphy **chron**ology **eco**logy **zo**ology

25. **medi** (middle) medial medi**an** **inter**mediate Medieval Medi**terr**anean

READING AND MEANINGS

(LESSONS 26-35, Student Reading Practice)

26. **nov (new)**   novel   novice   **in**novation   **re**novate

27. **nym, onym (name, word)** **syn**onym **ant**onym   **homo**nym   **an**onymous

28. **omni (all)**   omni**poten**t   omni**vor**e **pan (all)** pana**cea**   pan**orama**

29. **ped (foot, feet)**   pedal   pedestrian   **bi**ped   pedi**cure**

30. **pri, prim (first)**   prim**ary**   primitive   primate   prior**ity**

31. **tend, tens (stretch, strain)** **ex**tend   tense   intensity   **hyper**tension

32. **terr (land)** terrace   territory   **Medi**terranean   terr**arium**

33. **tract (draw, pull)**   tractor   **at**tract   **dis**tract   **ex**tract

34. **uni (one)**   united   uniform   uni**cycl**e   uni**son**

35. **vis, vid (see)**   vision   vis**ible**   **in**vis**ible**   video

Made in the USA
Middletown, DE
11 July 2018